The Which? Guide to Getting Married

About the author

Elizabeth Martyn is a freelance writer who has worked in women's magazines and publishing. She has written articles on a wide range of subjects and is author of several books, including the *Good Housekeeping Guide to Planning a Wedding* and the *Good Housekeeping Guide to Everyday Etiquette* (both Ebury Press) and a book on second marriages, *Second Time Around* (Optima).

The Which? Guide to Getting Married

Elizabeth Martyn

 CONSUMERS' ASSOCIATION

Which? Books are commissioned and researched by
Consumers' Association and published by
Which? Ltd, 2 Marylebone Road, London NW1 4DF
Email address: books@which.net

Distributed by The Penguin Group:
Penguin Books Ltd, 80 Strand, London WC2R 0RL

Acknowledgement to Virginia Wallis for Chapters 5, 21 and 22

First edition April 1999
Reprinted 2001
Revised edition 2002

British Library Cataloguing in Publication Data
A catalogue record for this book is available from the British Library

ISBN 0 85202 889 X

For a full list of *Which?* books, please write to Which? Books, Castlemead, Gascoyne Way, Hertford X, SG14 1LH or access our web site at www.which.net

Cover and text design by Kysen Creative Consultants
Cover photograph by Robert Harding Picture Library
Editorial and production: Joanna Bregosz, Vicky Fisher, Robert Gray, Mary Sunderland

Typeset by Saxon Graphics Ltd, Derby
Printed and bound in Great Britain by Clays Ltd, Bungay, Suffolk

Contents

	Introduction	7
1	Getting engaged	11
2	What kind of wedding?	20
3	Second marriages	30
4	Your wedding budget	35
5	Financing your wedding	50
6	Planning ahead	56
7	Using a computer to enhance your wedding	68
8	Principal players	74
9	Wedding guests	81
10	Wedding gifts	92
11	Wedding outfits	97
12	Flowers	109
13	Transport	119
14	Music and readings for the ceremony	123
15	Wedding cake options	131
16	Photographs and video	135
17	Civil ceremonies	143
18	Religious ceremonies	154
19	Organising the reception	167
20	At the reception	188
21	Insurance	202
22	Financing your future	209
	Appendix: Wedding law	218
	Addresses★	230
	Index	237

★ An asterisk next to the name of an organisation in the text indicates that the address can be found in this section

Introduction

Six out of every ten weddings in Britain take place in a civil rather than a religious setting. This move away from the traditional church wedding has been evident since the early 1990s, and one factor that has influenced it has been the availability in England and Wales, since 1995, of approved licensed premises. Around 2,500 venues such as hotels, stately homes, restaurants, castles, sports grounds and even the London Eye, have been licensed for the solemnisation of marriage.

This change has enabled couples to have a civil ceremony that mirrors a church ceremony in all but religious content. They can now personalise their ceremony by adding readings and music (as long as they are secular). Some couples take this a step further by arranging their wedding to reflect their surroundings – for example, by marrying in a castle in medieval dress or in a hotel in Bath with dress, transport and trappings in the style of a Jane Austen novel.

An increasing number of couples are choosing to get married abroad. This option enables them to escape the stress that can accompany a wedding at home, perhaps arising from family arguments or problems connected with divorced parents and step-families. Other couples simply like the idea of getting married somewhere exotic, while many choose to get married abroad because they can save money by having their wedding and honeymoon in the same place.

Those who want something a bit different might opt for, say, a quiet civil wedding in a register office followed by an alternative ceremony elsewhere, perhaps in their garden or on the shores of a lake or beside the sea. The choices open to these couples are unlimited because alternative ceremonies carry no legal weight and are therefore not subject to any restrictions (for example, a civil or religious ceremony in England and Wales must, to be legal, be held indoors).

So why are couples breaking with tradition? One reason is that people are marrying later in life. In 1999 the average age at marriage for a man was 34.4 years, and for a woman 31.8 years. About 70 per cent of couples have lived together before marrying and see the ceremony as a public confirmation of an existing commitment, rather than the forging of a new one. Couples who live together before marriage are more likely to choose a civil wedding than those who do not. Another factor is the number of second marriages. In 1999, four marriages out of every ten were remarriages for either one or both partners. With the current restrictions on marriage in church for those who have been divorced, a civil wedding is the only option for many of these couples. Many couples who are not religious feel that it would be hypocritical to have a traditional wedding in church; instead, they might opt for an elaborate civil wedding in, for example, a stately home. Other couples want more freedom to personalise their wedding and it is easier to do this with a civil wedding in an alternative venue than in a church. Finally, traditional weddings call for family unity: for example, parents are expected to sit together in church, stand together in a receiving line and sit together at the top table at the reception. An untraditional wedding, followed by an informal reception, where etiquette is not as rigid, can alleviate the tension of a traditional wedding format for couples whose parents are divorced and perhaps have remarried.

Preparing for marriage

No one marrying at the start of the twenty-first century can be unaware that in Britain more than two marriages out of every five end in divorce. Second marriages fail at an even higher rate than first ones. As a reflection of this, there are moves in England and Wales to legalise prenuptial contracts and introduce post-nuptial contracts.

Another response to the high divorce rate is to try preventative measures in a bid to help couples avoid becoming a statistic. In 2001, the government partially funded a publication encouraging couples to consider more carefully what they are entering into, which was given free to more than 250,000 couples applying to marry in register offices or the Church of England. Marriage preparation courses run by Relate* are available in some parts of the country, in which couples are asked to think about the major events that might happen during their marriage, such as parenthood, loss of employment or serious illness, and consider how these might impact on their relationship. The courses stress the importance of good communication (the lack of which is acknowledged to be at the root of most marital problems), and couples are shown how to achieve it. They are also made aware of the sorts of arguments that are likely to arise and are shown how best to contain and deal with these. Among the major causes of rows identified by Relate are money (number one on the list), attitudes to child-raising, arguments over the frequency of sex, and difficulties in agreeing over who does what around the house.

What this book covers

As couples are marrying later and have often already set up home together, an increasing number of them are arranging and paying for their wedding themselves. So the advice given in this book is aimed at the couple, rather than just the bride and her mother.

For the event to go without a hitch, detailed planning is crucial. Whether your wedding takes place in a village church, a synagogue, a register office or a Gothic castle, and whether you invite 50 or 150 guests, the organisation calls for strategy and forward thinking. As soon as you have agreed to marry, events take over and it is vital to keep on top of all the arrangements, to say nothing of the costs. This book will help you to plan every last detail, and checklists and budget sheets for you to copy and complete are provided throughout to help you to monitor your arrangements and spending. It gives information to those getting married for the second time, and examines plans of different styles of civil weddings, complete with timings and costs. The content of the civil ceremony is given in full, with suggestions for ways in which the basic ceremony may be personalised. Several religious ceremonies are also covered.

The guide takes a step-by-step approach to arranging the ceremony and reception. New for this edition is a chapter on the Internet; creating your own wedding website; and using a computer to keep track of plans, edit digital photographs and make your own stationery. The book also gives advice to couples on financing their wedding and their married future, with advice on tax, savings, investments, wills, pensions, life insurance and bank accounts.

Wedding etiquette

If you opt for a traditional white wedding, you need to be aware of the associated etiquette, from the wording of invitations to organisation of the seating plan and content of the speeches. All of it is in these pages but none of it is carved in stone, and you can mix the old rules with the new as you wish. Perhaps the bride wants to give a speech, or the groom would like his sister to act as 'best woman'. It can be done. Perhaps you are in a situation where traditional etiquette does not fit. Couples marrying for the second time, those who have children whom they would like to include, those whose parents are divorced or those who just want a very informal and personal occasion are at liberty to throw the rulebook to the winds and redesign the etiquette to suit themselves. After all, what do you give a couple who have already set up home and have lived together for some time? Where do you seat your stepchildren at the reception? And who stands in the receiving line when the bride's mother is there with her new husband and neither of them is on speaking terms with the bride's father? These questions, and many others, are answered in this guide. But all these factors pale into insignificance beside the real purpose of your wedding day, which is simply to make a public declaration of your mutual love and commitment.

Chapter 1

Getting engaged

For most people, becoming engaged to be married is a big step, not to be taken lightly. Whether you will be leaving your parents' home for the first time, you have been living with your partner for years or you are marrying for the second time, the decision to tie the knot is a momentous and exciting one. Although some couples dispense with any trappings of formal engagement, for most the time leading up to the wedding is one when they can enjoy making plans together and start getting used to the idea of a long-term shared future.

Announcing the news

Courtesy and tradition demand that you should first tell the bride's parents, who will, after all, probably make a financial contribution to the wedding. Ideally, you should visit them together unless long distance means that a phone call is the only option. The man does not need to ask his fiancée's father for permission to marry her, although he might like to do so as a mark of respect and consideration for his future father-in-law, if it seems appropriate. Whether you ask permission or not, the bride's parents will welcome a chance to talk to you together about your plans for the future. Next, you should tell the groom's parents – again, in person if you can. After that other family members and friends can be notified by phone or letter. If you decide to create your own wedding website (see pages 70–1) you can include details on the site of how you got engaged, the ring and so on.

Formal announcements

An announcement in the local paper or in one of the nationals is a good way to spread the news. Ring the 'Births, Deaths and Marriages' column a week or so before you want the announcement to appear. You may be able to send copy by email if you wish.

Traditionally, the bride's parents announce their daughter's engagement, but couples who live independently of their parents, or who are marrying for the second time, might prefer to make the announcement themselves. Standard formal wording is as follows, but you will see other versions in the engagements columns in any newspaper.

Mr G R Evans and Miss L A Thompson
The engagement is announced between Graham Ralph, younger son of Mr and Mrs Anthony Evans of Guildford, Surrey, and Lesley Anne, only daughter of Mr and Mrs Malcolm Thompson of Reigate, Surrey.

In the version below, the groom's father is deceased and his mother has not remarried:
... between Graham Ralph, younger son of the late Mr Anthony Evans and Mrs Martha Evans of Guildford, Surrey ...

In this version, the groom's mother has remarried:
... between Graham Ralph, younger son of the late Mr Anthony Evans and Mrs Martha Morgan of London ...

If the bride's parents have divorced but neither has remarried, it would say:
... Lesley Anne, only daughter of Mr Malcolm Thompson of Reigate, Surrey and Mrs Susan Thompson of Winchester, Hampshire.

If the bride's parents have divorced and the mother has remarried, it would read:
... Lesley Anne, only daughter of Mr Malcolm Thompson of Reigate, Surrey and Mrs James Wallace of Winchester, Hampshire.

An informal announcement (usually in a local newspaper), made by the couple themselves, could be:
Mr G R Evans and Miss L A Thompson
Graham Evans and Lesley Thompson are delighted to announce their engagement.

Engagement party

You might like to have a party or gathering of some kind to mark your engagement and to introduce your fiancé(e) to friends and family who have not yet met him or her. This could take any form you like, from a drinks party or a sit-down dinner to a night out at a club. You could also use it as an opportunity to announce your engagement, if you can arrange the party before the news gets around. Whether you have a party or not, you will probably receive some engagement gifts, and you should send a thank-you letter for these immediately from you both.

Introducing the parents

If the two sets of parents have not already met, then you should do your best to set up a meeting as soon as possible. You could arrange a lunch, dinner, or even a weekend stay if they live far apart. If you are planning a lavish wedding you will almost certainly be looking to both sets of parents for financial help, and this initial meeting would be a good time to start the all-important discussions about the wedding budget and who will pay for what (see pages 36–7). However, if a meeting is impossible, then an exchange of letters between the two sets of parents would help to reduce any feeling that they are meeting as strangers on the wedding day.

Choosing engagement and wedding rings

An engagement ring, though not compulsory, is a symbol of love and commitment that many couples enjoy choosing together. The range of styles is enormous so you should first decide on a price limit, then browse round a few jewellers' windows to get an idea of what is on offer.

The classic engagement ring, with a diamond solitaire, is still the most popular style. The cut of the diamond (the number of facets) is important because the more facets the diamond has, the more it will sparkle. The 'carat' value, which in diamonds is a measure of weight, is reflected in the price, and the heavier and larger the diamond, the more expensive it will be. The very finest, and most expensive, diamonds are completely clear and flawless, but stones with tiny flaws, visible only under magnification, can still be very beautiful and are cheaper. However, you do not need to restrict your choice to diamonds. The other precious stones – emeralds, rubies and sapphires – as well as a wide range of semi-precious stones, from agates and aquamarines to topaz and turquoise, are all beautiful and can either be set alone or in combination with diamonds. Some brides choose an engagement ring which incorporates their birthstone.

Birthstones

Month	Stone	Meaning
January	garnet (dark red)	constancy
February	amethyst (clear purple)	sincerity
March	aquamarine (pale blue/green) or bloodstone (green, flecked red)	courage (bloodstone)
April	diamond	love, innocence
May	emerald	happiness, hope
June	pearl	health and beauty
July	ruby	love and contentment
August	peridot (greenish yellow) or sardonyx (white/yellow layers)	married bliss (sardonyx)
September	sapphire	wisdom
October	opal (milky white/multi flecks)	hope
November	topaz	fidelity
December	turquoise	harmony

Gold and other metals

When used in rings, gold, which in its pure form is too soft for daily wear, is alloyed with other metals. The 'carat' value of gold refers to its purity, so 18-carat gold is purer and darker in colour than 9-carat, but also less durable. Most wedding rings are made of 18-carat gold, but people who do heavy work may choose a tougher 9-carat ring. White gold, which is alloyed with silver, is another popular choice, and rings are also available in matt gold and rose gold as well as in combinations of colours.

Platinum, a beautiful silver-coloured and very hard-wearing metal, is also available and is more expensive than gold. Silver is cheaper than either gold or platinum but is less hard wearing. It tarnishes and will start to wear thin over the years and show signs of knocks and scratches.

What type of design?

The choice is wide, and you may well be able to find exactly what you want in a high-street jeweller's, particularly if you are looking for a traditional setting. If you do not see anything you like, you can have a ring made for you. You can either choose one of the jeweller's existing designs or have one made up to your own specification, using the stones and metals you particularly want, although this is a more expensive option. Antique rings can be very attractive and often have dainty settings and unusual combinations of stones. Go to a reputable antique dealer and get the ring checked by a valuer before buying it. One other option is to wear a family engagement ring. If it is too large or small, a jeweller can adjust it to fit you.

Almost all women, and 80 per cent of men, wear a wedding ring, and the traditional plain gold band, which comes in a variety of widths, colours and cuts, remains highly popular. For something different, however, look for engagement and wedding ring sets, where the two rings are designed to match, and may interlock. A plain band studded with diamonds or other gems can double as engagement and wedding ring; or you could choose a Russian wedding ring, with three interlinked gold bands of different colours, a cladagh (clasped hands) ring or signet ring.

Rings can be engraved inside with your wedding date, initials or any short wording you choose. This usually takes four to six weeks.

Tips for choosing the perfect rings

- Remember, you will wear the rings for the rest of your life. A high-fashion ring might seem like fun now but could look sadly dated in 20 years' time.

- Try on lots of different rings to find the weight and style that suits you. Something that looks great in the jeweller's window may look quite wrong on your finger.
- Choose engagement and wedding rings that are made of the same metal and carat, otherwise they may wear each other down as they rub together.
- Make sure the rings fit well. If you buy on a hot or cold day your finger measurement may not be a true gauge of fit.
- Take time to choose and keep an open mind. The right rings will give you daily pleasure, so it is worth taking care when you choose.

Q *Can a man wear an engagement ring?*

A Yes he can wear an engagement ring, an engagement/wedding ring set to match the woman's, a signet ring or any other sort you choose. Otherwise, you could give him a wedding ring that can be worn on a different finger until the wedding day. Some men do not like wearing rings, in which case he could have another item that he can wear all the time, such as a neck chain or watch.

Caring for your rings

Engagement rings with intricate settings can quickly pick up grime and grease, and stones lose their sparkle with daily wear. When buying the ring, check with the jeweller which is the best way to clean it, as some stones are particularly delicate and should not be immersed in cleaning liquids. Always be gentle when cleaning and have the settings checked occasionally. Some jewellers will steam-clean your ring while you wait.

Many people like to wear their wedding ring all the time, but engagement rings should be taken off when doing rough chores to avoid damaging them or scratching delicate surfaces in the home. Rings with 'rub-over' settings, where the gems are set flush with the band rather than standing proud, can take more everyday wear and tear than some other designs.

Remember to add your rings to your household contents insurance (see Chapter 21). A costly ring could be worth more than the single-item limit, which in many policies is £1,000, and should be itemised separately on the policy and covered at all times, not just when in your home. When you buy your ring, ask for a valuation certificate and keep it safely, together with a photograph of the ring(s) if possible, as it will be needed if you ever need to make a claim. Valuations need to be re-done every three to five years, otherwise insurance companies may not accept them.

Alternatives to engagement rings

If you do not want to wear an engagement ring, you could choose another piece of jewellery, such as a necklace, locket or bracelet, instead, or spend the money on something for your home. Remember, though, if it is cost that is putting you off, that it is not the price of the ring that is important, but what it stands for. The ring may have been inexpensive but will still be a potent and treasured reminder of your partner and your relationship.

Prenuptial agreements

Prenuptial agreements – contracts signed by couples before they marry – once the province of the rich and famous, have become widely used in Europe and the United States, but are not legally binding in England and Wales. The prime function of a prenuptial agreement is to itemise the division of assets in the event of a divorce, but it can also include expectations in regard to sharing the responsibilities of housework, childcare and so on.

As long ago as 1998 the present government mooted plans to legalise prenuptial agreements in England and Wales, on the grounds that they could help to cut down on costly divorce litigation. No progress has been made on legalising prenuptial contracts since then, partly because many high-court family division judges responded unenthusiastically to the idea, believing that to allow such agreements would introduce an underlying idea of divorce from the outset of a marriage. The Church, too, criticised the plan, saying that such agreements weaken, rather than strengthen marriage, by encouraging couples to view divorce as an option, when they should see marriage as a life-long commitment. A minority of judges are in favour of the idea of prenuptial contracts, however, and think that courts should honour them, provided they have been fairly entered into, with separate legal advice given to both parties, and full disclosure of both sides' assets, subject to the interests of any children of the marriage.

Even though a change in the law is not planned at the moment, it is possible that prenuptial agreements could be legalised retrospectively at some time in the future. For a small fee you can download a prenuptial agreement from a legal website such as Desktop Lawyer*, and this is the kind of document that would be required if the law were called upon to enforce your contract in the future. Before you embark on any discussions, be aware that prenuptial agreements of any type can arouse powerful emotions, and couples have been known to call off the marriage because the negotiations involved in making arrangements over the future division of assets caused too much bad feeling between them.

Every couple will have to decide for themselves whether some kind of prenuptial agreement has any place in their relationship. Whether or not they want to draw up a formal document, all couples would be well advised to discuss the way they see their future lives together taking shape. Talking over questions such as whether you both want children, how you plan to manage spending and saving, who will take responsibility for what in the home and for the care of any children you have, can help to clarify differences of attitude and might avoid problems later on.

While many people are happy to marry in the expectation of a life-long tie, where problems will be resolved as and when they occur, others find that discussion (or even making a written agreement) helps to focus their thoughts and highlight exactly what is involved when entering into a marriage.

If the engagement is broken off

However upset and embarrassed you may be about breaking off an engagement, remember that it is easier to unpick a wedding than it is to unravel a marriage. It is very common to have occasional doubts as the wedding approaches; almost everyone suffers from last-minute nerves or the urge to escape from the pressure. But if your fears are more serious and persist even during the enjoyable parts of the preparations, it is far better to talk your concerns over with your partner and halt the proceedings, even if only for a short time.

If you do decide to break off the engagement, you do not need to give any explanations. Relatives and friends can be informed quietly, and if you originally placed an announcement in the newspaper, a brief notice of cancellation is all that is needed, simply stating your names and the fact that the marriage will not now take place.

Traditionally, if the woman breaks off the engagement, she should return her ring to the man. If he breaks the engagement, then she may keep the ring, although she may prefer to return it. Any presents the couple have received should be returned to the givers.

Chapter 2

What kind of wedding?

One of the first decisions you need to make is whether you would like to have a civil or religious ceremony. Couples with a religious background who want their church's sanction on their marriage will naturally choose a religious ceremony, as will those who want a traditional wedding. However, there are many reasons why nearly two-thirds of couples choose a civil ceremony, and these are discussed below. You may have to take the thoughts and feelings of your families into consideration but ultimately you should choose the type of ceremony you both want.

Once you have made your choice, you can go on to consider where the wedding will take place. As a result of the 1994 Marriage Act the range of options for civil marriages in England and Wales has increased beyond the register office to include a wide selection of other approved premises (see opposite). However, if you are having a religious marriage then your choice will probably be limited to either of your parish churches. How informal/formal you want your wedding to be and roughly how many guests you want – and can afford – to invite will both influence the sorts of places you can choose for the ceremony.

Civil weddings

Nearly two-thirds of all weddings are civil ceremonies, that is those which take place in a register office or other authorised place. Although the wording used differs from that in a religious ceremony, a civil wedding can be just as solemn and meaningful as a religious one (see page 144 for full details of the civil service).

You might choose a civil wedding because you have no religious beliefs, and feel that marrying in church would be meaningless or hypocritical. Perhaps your beliefs differ to the extent that a religious wedding is impossible. If one or both partners are divorced, then arranging a church wedding may be difficult (see page 32 for details). Some people opt for a civil wedding because they want a quieter, less lavish wedding than is sometimes involved in religious proceedings, although this is not to say that civil weddings have to be low key.

Some religious ceremonies, for instance Hindu and Sikh, usually take place in premises that are not licensed for the solemnisation of marriages, and so the couple must by law have a civil ceremony as well. (See the Appendix for legal requirements.)

Register offices

Most civil weddings take place in register offices. To find out where your local register office is, look under Registration of Births, Deaths and Marriages in the phone book. You are not tied to your local office however, and may marry in any office in England or Wales, provided you live in either country. Some register offices are in beautiful buildings and are much more appealing than others, so if this is important to you, hunt around before deciding. Many local authorities have smartened up their marriage rooms, and all are now committed to customer care and providing a high level of service. Your local authority may have a website with details of all register offices in your area, plus information about options for the ceremony.

You will probably be allowed to personalise your ceremony with readings or music, but check with the superintendent registrar beforehand. No religious content is allowed in any additions you make to the ceremony.

Approved licensed premises

A civil wedding in England and Wales does not have to take place in a register office. Around 2,500 venues have been licensed, and you can marry in a hotel, country inn, stately home or castle, or even in the boardroom of a football club, in a museum or on the London Eye. Approved licensed venues are not yet available in Scotland, although there are moves to bring legislation in line with that south of the border in the future. At the moment, however, your only option for a civil wedding in Scotland is the register office.

Your local register office should be able to tell you about licensed premises in your immediate area, or a list of them all is available from the Office for National Statistics★. For more details of each place, including capacity and catering arrangements, refer to *Noble's Wedding Venues Guide* (see Publications, page 235).

Restrictions on approved premises

More venues are becoming licensed all the time. To gain a licence the premises must:

- be open to the public (so your own home could not be licensed)
- be indoors (so weddings cannot take place in the open air)
- be fixed, so a ship, for instance, would have to be permanently moored. It is not possible to marry on board a ship while it is at sea
- be suitably solemn.

If the venue of your dreams does not meet these criteria – perhaps you want to marry beside a lake, in a ruined abbey, or simply in your own garden – then you could consider having a civil ceremony in a register office, followed by an 'alternative' ceremony at your chosen venue (see page 28 and page 151).

Advantages of a wedding at an approved venue

- Where register offices are generally small, and can seldom accommodate more than a handful of guests, approved premises tend to be larger, and some can hold up to several hundred people, so all your family and friends can be present at the ceremony.
- The ceremony and reception can take place at the same venue, so there's no break in the proceedings while people travel from one to another.
- Approved premises offer more flexible hours than register offices, and you should be able to book them for a whole day on a Saturday, and even on a Sunday or Bank Holiday, although you would need to persuade the registrars to attend.

- The proceedings can be given a more traditional feel than is usually possible in a register office. For instance, the bride may be able to enter to music, and walk down an aisle to join the groom. She can wear a white wedding dress, which sometimes looks out of place in a register office, and have a retinue of attendants which the space available in most register offices would not allow.
- You may be able to personalise your ceremony to a greater extent at an approved venue than at a register office, by adding more readings, live music, and even your own words to the service (see pages 128–130 for more details). Once again, however, no religious content is allowed.

Themed weddings

Your wedding could be themed to suit the setting. A castle or country house could provide the perfect backdrop for a medieval, 1930s or Jane Austen-style wedding. You could either restrict the costumes to the bridal party or encourage your guests to join in by dressing up too. Other options are to pick a simpler theme, and let a particular colour combination run through the day, making it easier for guests to take part; or let the season dictate the mood of your wedding and have a Christmas or springtime theme, with decorations, music and a cake chosen to tie in.

Religious weddings

The religious ceremony is imbued with ritual and tradition, the surroundings are solemn and often beautiful, and the wording of the religious ceremonies encompasses ideas of mutual love, fidelity, harmony and stability.

In the Anglican church you have the right to marry in your parish church as long as neither of you has a former marriage partner still living and one of you lives within the parish boundaries. Most ministers will expect you to attend services and preparation sessions to ensure that you understand the religious significance of the marriage service.

In England and Wales a religious ceremony may be conducted only in a church. In Scotland, however, it is the celebrant who is licensed, not the premises, and a religious ceremony may take place anywhere – at your home, on a river bank, in a historical building – as long as the minister agrees that the surroundings are suitable.

A Roman Catholic priest will expect you to be confirmed and may insist on a lengthy period (usually six months) of notice of your intention to marry as it is regarded as essential for you to prepare properly for such a serious commitment. (See the Appendix for legal requirements.)

Interfaith marriages

Some religions do not allow marriage to members of different religions. If you suspect there may be a problem make enquiries immediately, since if no compromise can be found you may be forced to have a civil ceremony.

- There is no objection to marriage between people of different religions if you belong to the **Church of England**, **Church of Scotland**, **Church in Wales** or **Nonconformist (or Free Church)**, such as **Methodist, Baptist or United Reformed**.
- A **Roman Catholic** must acquire a special dispensation from his or her priest in order to marry a baptised Christian from another church. A priest's dispensation is also needed if the marriage is to take place in a non-Catholic church. If a Roman Catholic wishes to marry a non-baptised Christian, or someone who has no faith, then a bishop's dispensation will be needed; your priest will know how to obtain this. The couple may be required to take a course of instruction on marriage and agree to do everything in their power to bring up their children in the Roman Catholic faith.
- In the **Jewish faith**, if either the bride or groom is not Jewish, he or she must convert before getting married. This could take two years or more, depending on whether the conversion takes place under the Orthodox, Reform or Liberal/Progressive authority. Conversion is complicated and demanding, involving instruction and an examination.
- **Quakers** require that a non-member who wants to marry a Quaker meet with at least two members of the Religious Society of Friends,★ so that they can assess whether the person has sufficient understanding of the religious nature of the society for the marriage to be allowed.

Getting married abroad

Tying the knot in an exotic foreign location is becoming increasingly popular, with about 17,000 couples a year marrying abroad. Many people who get married abroad do so because they want a quiet ceremony without the stress that accompanies a wedding in the UK. Also, if the ceremony and the honeymoon are in the same place, the cost is much less than the average UK wedding. The choice of destinations is wide, and many major tour operators now have dedicated wedding brochures and telephone numbers (see page 234). Although it is possible to organise a wedding abroad yourself, most people use a tour organiser, who can offer a complete package. You can either stay on at your wedding resort for your honeymoon or choose a two-centre package, if you prefer.

Exotic wedding venues

If you would like a beach wedding, your choice of destinations could include: the Caribbean, Kenya, Mexico, Sri Lanka, the Seychelles, Mauritius, Hawaii and Thailand. In the USA you could get married in a chapel of love in Las Vegas – with an Elvis look-a-like singing during the ceremony – or have a fantasy wedding in Disneyland, with Mickey Mouse as a guest. The truly adventurous might like an underwater wedding at Key Largo or marriage in a helicopter 1,000 feet above Orlando. Other options include a slope-side wedding in a ski resort, a ceremony in a game reserve in Africa or even a marriage on the Equator.

The legal requirements vary from country to country with regard to minimum residency required, documents needed and so on. See page 227 for preliminary guidance on this, but be sure to check carefully with the tour operator, who will be able to give you a detailed checklist of what is needed. Some countries will not marry people of certain denominations or those who have been divorced, so do check carefully before making any bookings. A marriage performed abroad in accordance with local law is valid in the UK as long as you would both have been legally entitled to marry in the UK. Check on the availability of a marriage certificate, as you may have to take steps to register your marriage in the UK in order to get a duplicate certificate, should you ever need one. Your travel company should be able to advise on this.

Limitations of getting married abroad

Although wedding packages are very popular, they can be basic. The standard package usually offers all the paperwork, a simple ceremony, a bottle of sparkling wine, a posy of flowers and a few photographs. If you want something more lavish, choose a company that offers a good range of extras, which might include special transport, floral decorations, extra champagne, a video and more photographs, and a celebration dinner, but be prepared to pay extra for all of these.

- If all you want is a simple ceremony with no extras, and you would have taken a foreign honeymoon anyway, getting married abroad can be an inexpensive choice, with the basic ceremony package ranging from £200 to £700, excluding the cost of the holiday.
- In popular resorts there may be several weddings each day, and you may have to queue for a licence. Tour operators can advise on less busy destinations.
- A beach ceremony can be very simple and brief; this is fine if that is what you want and you know what to expect.
- Although you might be longing for a quiet wedding with none of the hassle of guest lists and seating plans, your family and friends may feel left out. Some companies will organise a special deal for guests who want to travel with you and will even arrange to put them up at a different hotel so that you have some privacy. Alternatively, you could organise a blessing or a celebratory party when you return home.
- Photographs taken at a wedding abroad may not be of such a high standard as those you would get at home.

Marrying a foreigner

If one of you comes from a country other than the UK, you will have to take various steps when organising the wedding. These will depend on the country in which you plan to marry (check with the relevant consulate).

An Anglo-Japanese wedding

Mark and Yumiko met in Osaka while he was travelling round the world before going to university. After living together for 18 months they returned to England and later went back to Japan to get married.

Yumiko's parents did all the organisation for the wedding. First, the couple were driven to a Japanese register office for a civil ceremony, which would be recognised under UK law. After this they were taken to a specialist dresser, who arranged Yumiko's hair in a traditional style, applied white make-up to her face and helped both Yumiko and Mark to dress in traditional kimonos. They were then taken to a Shinto temple for the traditional ceremony conducted by a Shinto priest. This was in Japanese, but Yumiko's mother had arranged for a translator to be present so that the English guests could understand what was being said. The couple sat side by side in the centre, with eight members of Mark's family – who had flown to Japan for the occasion – on one side. As a sign of courtesy towards Mark's family, only eight members of Yumiko's family sat on the other side. The couple did not have to do or say anything during the ceremony.

After the ceremony the two families went back to a nearby hotel where the couple got changed into more comfortable clothes before sharing an elaborate meal with their guests.

In the United Kingdom
A foreigner will generally be asked to produce a passport as identification when applying to marry in the UK. He or she should take steps to ensure that a UK marriage will be valid in his or her country of origin; the consulate will be able to advise on this.

In a foreigner's country of origin
To be married in a foreign country under the law of that country, a UK subject may be required to give notice of the intended marriage in England, Wales, Scotland or Northern Ireland, if that is where he or she is resident, or to the marriage officer of the country in which he or she lives, and then apply for a certificate saying that no impediment to the marriage exists. It is important for the individual to check with the consulate that the marriage will be recognised in the

UK. The rules on this vary widely from country to country, so check carefully.

Alternative ceremonies

Those who find a religious service inappropriate and the civil ceremony uninspiring might like to consider an alternative ceremony. These are not legally binding, so you would need to have a civil ceremony as well, but the alternative service could be the main part of the wedding, to which most guests are invited, and could take place in any setting you choose.

Among the possibilities are Pagan, Druid, New Age, Viking, Spiritualist and Humanist ceremonies, or you could create a ceremony that is entirely your own. A number of books give plenty of ideas for you to think about (see Publications, page 235). For more details of what form an alternative ceremony might take, see pages 151–3.

One couple wrote their own wedding promises

Jane and Michael had a very quiet register office wedding, followed by a reception for friends and relatives. They had worked out between themselves a list of ten 'wedding promises' and after the speeches they stood side by side and read these out alternately. The final promise was 'never to argue when tired'. A relative had produced a decorative copy of the promises on her computer and had it framed as a wedding present for the couple; it now hangs in their kitchen and is a daily reminder of the promises they wrote and made together.

Celebrating gay and lesbian relationships

UK law, unlike that of Denmark, the Netherlands, Norway, Sweden, France and Germany, does not recognise same-sex partnerships. However, in 2001 the Greater London Authority* introduced the London Partnerships Register. Same-sex couples can have their relationships officially recognised, and declare their commitment to each other by signing the register in a ceremony at the Visitors' Centre of the Greater London Authority. Legislation is due to be introduced to set up partnership registers nationwide.

The register does not confer any legal rights, but parliamentary bills currently in the pipeline would, if they become law, give legal recognition to civilly recognised same-sex relationships under specific areas of law including inheritance tax, pensions and social security.

There are other possibilities for gay and lesbian couples who would like to mark their relationship with some sort of ceremony. The Lesbian and Gay Christian Movement★ can provide details of ministers who are willing to conduct blessing ceremonies for lesbian and gay couples. The Unitarian and Free Christian Church★ has a tradition of supporting civil and religious liberty, and can put you in touch with a minister who could organise a service for you. Celebrations of commitment have been held by local meetings of The Religious Society of Friends★ (Quakers), but in order to participate couples need to be involved in the local Quaker community and in sympathy with its religious principles. For a non-religious ceremony, the Pink Triangle Trust★ can arrange an affirmation ceremony which gives the couple the opportunity to make pledges of love and commitment and exchange rings.

Chapter 3

Second marriages

The number of second marriages is increasing, and more than 40 per cent of marriages are not the first for either one or both partners. Much of the information given in this book is just as applicable to those planning a second wedding as to those planning a first. However, couples marrying for a subsequent time are far more likely to choose a civil setting and may also have children from previous marriages to consider when planning the day. Couples who are remarrying often dispense with, or alter, some of the traditional wedding trappings to suit the occasion. Hints on how to do this are given here, while the Appendix has information on the legal requirements concerning second marriages.

Before the wedding

Among the first people to know of your intention to marry should be any children of your previous marriages. You will know best how to break the news, and how it is likely to be received. It's important that children hear the news from you, and not accidentally from anyone else.

If you want to make a formal announcement in the press, it can be made by the bride's parents if you want to follow this tradition, or you can make the announcement yourselves. See page 12 for wordings. If the woman is known by her previous married name, as she may be if she has children from her former marriage, this can be used in announcements:

Mr P W Wilcott and Mrs S E Adams
Peter Wilcott and Serena Adams are delighted to announce their engagement.

Changing your surname

If a woman has children from a previous marriage who will be living with the newly married couple, she may wish to retain her previous married name or to change the children's surname to her new married name. This is a sensitive issue, which should be discussed with all parties involved, including the children and their father, if possible, before taking any action. Other options for changing/not changing your name, and details of who to inform of any change, are on page 64.

Considering the financial implications of remarriage

It is a sad fact that second marriages are more likely to end in failure than first. Without wishing to take a negative approach, it is certainly sensible to give careful consideration to your financial affairs before you remarry. A few couples decide to have a pre- or post-nuptial agreement (see page 17), which sets out what should happen to your mutual finances and property in the event of a separation. Even if this approach does not appeal, you should study the financial implications of remarriage, especially if either or both of you have children from a previous relationship. It is especially important to make a will in this situation, as marriage invalidates previous wills. See Chapter 22 for more details on this, and other aspects of financial planning.

What kind of wedding?

The majority of people who are marrying for the second time choose a civil setting, and are more likely to wed in approved licensed premises rather than a register office than those marrying for the first time. Using approved premises provides the opportunity to have a celebratory occasion with many of the frills usually associated with religious ceremonies. Another possibility to make your wedding day extra special, is to have a quiet register office marriage, followed by an alternative ceremony in which you can, if you wish, include a religious element. See Chapter 17 for more details on different types of civil ceremonies and alternative ceremonies.

If you wish, a civil ceremony can be followed by a church blessing (see overleaf). Talk to your vicar before making any arrangements, as some do not approve of hymns, bridesmaids, flowers and traditional bridal dress at a blessing.

If you are hoping for a religious wedding however, this may prove hard or impossible to arrange. While the Church of England is happy to remarry widows or widowers, the question of whether or not a divorced person may remarry in church is a cloudy one. Church regulations currently forbid it, but it seems that some ministers flout this rule and will agree to marry people who are divorced, especially if they consider that the people involved are not badly at fault over the collapse of their first marriages.

In Scotland divorcees may marry in church at the discretion of the minister, who will want to know something of the circumstances of the breakdown of any previous marriages before agreeing. See the Appendix for further information about remarriage.

Church of England service of blessing for second marriages

This service takes place in church after the couple have had a civil marriage. Since it is not a marriage service there is no need for banns to be called nor for the register to be signed. Unlike a marriage ceremony, there is no residency requirement, so couples may seek a blessing at a church other than that of their own parish.

At the beginning of the service the couple to be blessed come into the church together without ceremony and sit at the front of the church. The minister leads some prayers and there may be readings, hymns or psalms and a sermon. The couple then stand and the minister says to them both:

'N and N, you have committed yourselves to each other in marriage and your marriage is recognised by law. The Church of Christ understands marriage to be, in the will of God, the union of a man and a woman, for better, for worse, for richer, for poorer, in sickness and in health, to love and to cherish, till parted by death. Is this your understanding of the covenant and promise that you have made?

The couple respond: *'It is.'*

The minister then asks the couple in turn: *'N, have you resolved to be faithful to your wife/husband, forsaking all others, so long as you both shall live?'*

The man and then the woman respond in turn: *'That is my resolve, with the help of God.'*

Rings are not exchanged during the service, but rings which were given during the civil ceremony may be blessed. The hand(s) wearing the ring(s) should be extended towards the minister, who says:

'*Heavenly Father, by your blessing let this ring/these rings be to N and N a symbol of unending love and faithfulness and of the promises they have made to each other; through Jesus Christ our Lord. Amen.*'
The minister then turns to the congregation and says to them:
'*N and N have here affirmed their Christian understanding and resolve in the marriage which they have begun. Will you their relatives and friends do all in your power to uphold them in their marriage?*'
The congregation respond: '*We will.*'

More prayers and hymns follow before the end of the service, which may also include holy communion.

Preparing for the wedding day

Whether or not you choose to invite a former spouse to your wedding will depend on your circumstances and how appropriate you feel it would be for him or her to be present. Children of a former marriage are usually invited, and other members of your ex-spouse's family could be included if you think it is appropriate.

Invitations can be sent traditionally, as from the bride's parents, or, more usually, from the bride and groom themselves. See page 88 for wordings. Family and friends will want to give wedding gifts, even if you have been established in your home(s) for some years. See page 94 for ideas of what to ask for. What you wear depends on where you get married, and your own inclinations. There is nothing to stop the bride wearing a traditional white wedding dress, particularly if the wedding takes place in approved premises where more formal clothes won't look out of place. For other suggestions of what to wear, see Chapter 11.

The bride can be given away by her father and have bridesmaids and pages, or the ceremony can be kept simple, involving just the couple and two witnesses. You can have a best man or not, as you wish.

Involving your children in your wedding

Some couples who opt for a civil wedding have children from a previous marriage whom they would like to give a special role on the day. If the children are over 18 you could ask them to witness your marriage. Younger teenagers could be entrusted with your ring(s), producing them for you at the appropriate part of the ceremony. Small children can act as attendants, and wear traditional bridesmaid's or page's clothes and carry flowers, or be dressed in their party regalia if you prefer to be less formal. They can be seated directly behind you during the ceremony if space permits, or in the front row of guests. Most couples choose not to invite the other parent of the children, no matter how well they all get on, and so you will need to ask another family member or friend to keep an eye on little ones while the ceremony takes place.

After the ceremony, children can be given their own boxes of confetti to scatter either near the register office, or elsewhere.

The reception

Full information on organising a reception is given in Chapters 19 and 20. Whether or not you have a traditional receiving line depends on whether you have organised the wedding yourselves or had some help and financial input from parents, and also on how formal you want to be. If you are having a sit-down meal, you can follow the traditional seating plan if you wish, or adapt it to suit your own family needs, for instance by including your children on the top table if you wish. The best advice is to organise things so that everyone feels comfortable.

Speeches at second marriages

The speeches are usually less formal, and the bride's father does not have to make a speech, as he will probably not have given his daughter away. He may propose a toast to the bride and groom, or the toast may be proposed by another friend or relative. Traditionally this would be a man, but there is no reason why a woman could not make the speech if you prefer. The groom responds to the toast with thanks on behalf of himself and his new wife. It is inappropriate in either speech to mention previous marriages.

Chapter 4

Your wedding budget

Getting married usually involves major expenditure, with the average cost of a traditional white wedding being about £13,000 (including the honeymoon). So before you start spending, decide how much you can afford and plan your budget carefully. If you do not, you will almost certainly find that you overrun your limit. See Chapter 5 for more details on financing your wedding.

The preliminary budget

If you take the time to plan your budget carefully, you will almost certainly save money. Make a long list – or copy and use the one in this book – of every conceivable item that will be needed for your wedding day. Be it large or small, put it in your preliminary budget and write a figure against it. Phone round suppliers, browse through wedding magazines, trawl the shops, compare estimates (but remember, these are not binding) to get an idea of how much each item costs (we give a guideline in this book – see pages 39–49).

When you have some idea of what to allow for each item, add it all up and include a contingency amount of 5 to 10 per cent of the total cost for unforeseen expenses. It is important to include this sum since it will almost certainly be needed and should not be viewed as an optional extra. For example, if your absolute top limit is £10,000, you should work to a budget of £9,000, allowing for a 10 per cent contingency of £1,000.

At this point, if the total is more than you can afford, you may have to rethink your plans and cut out some items to meet your limit. For example, you could have two bridesmaids instead of six, opt for a paying bar at your reception instead of providing all the alcohol yourselves, or invite fewer guests. Do not be tempted to underestimate deliberately.

Who pays for what?

You will also need to work out who is going to pay for what. The traditional responsibilities are shown in the box below but nowadays few families stick rigidly to tradition, and instead apportion the cost to suit themselves.

In a great many cases the couple themselves foot a sizeable proportion of the bill, although the bride's family is still likely to pay for more than the groom's family. Try to sit everyone down together as soon as you have a rough idea of the amounts involved and work out where each cost will be borne. This may not be as easy as it

---

Traditional responsibility for payment

The bride's family pays for:
- engagement announcements (in the newspapers)
- invitations and all other wedding stationery
- the bride's clothing
- the bridesmaids' outfits (but often the bridesmaids, or their parents, will pay)
- flowers in the church and at the reception
- photographs/video
- transport to church/wedding venue and reception for the bridal party
- wedding cake
- the reception

The groom (or his family) pays for:
- engagement and wedding rings (bride pays for groom's ring)
- cost of licence or registrar's fee
- all church expenses
- transport to church/wedding venue for groom and best man
- bride's and bridesmaids' flowers, buttonholes
- gifts for attendants
- hotel for first night
- honeymoon

---

sounds, and you may have to use considerable diplomacy to arrive at a point where everyone is happy and no one feels unfairly burdened with his or her share of the cost.

The final budget

Once you have agreed on the limit for expenditure on your wedding (and the cost of individual items), you can start placing firm orders.

- Wherever possible get **written quotations** – which are legally binding – and ask for them to be made out in as much detail as possible. If you change your mind about anything you have asked for, confirm in writing.
- Keep careful **records of all expenditure**. File away all bills, receipts and so on and do not throw anything away. Keep notes of any deposits paid, when the final balance is due and how much it is.
- Consider opening a **wedding bank account**, so that all cheques come from a single source.
- It is very **easy to overrun your budget**. Keep yours on a tight rein by being aware that any extras – and you will be offered dozens – will add to the cost, and a few relatively small amounts can add up to a sizeable total.
- Naturally, you will change your mind about things and discover **items that were not in your original budget**. Look at the impact on the overall budget before adding anything.

___

'The hotel tried to overcharge'

When Susanna and Andrew booked their reception, months before the wedding, they were told that payment in full was expected a few days before the event. When the final bill came, it included a charge of £450 for the use of the (big) room. Fortunately, during their original visit Susanna had taken a checklist and against 'separate room charge?' she had recorded 'no'. The new hotel manager was not happy (remember that staff can change between the booking and the actual occasion – another good reason for keeping detailed records) but was forced to accept the situation. However, it was a stressful and unpleasant incident, which the couple could have done without just a few days before their wedding.

___

Negotiating discounts

It is quite often possible to get a discount on items for your wedding. Try offering the full amount at the time of ordering, in return for, say, 10 per cent off, but be aware that if the company runs into financial problems before delivering, your money could be at risk. The late autumn, winter and early spring are relatively quiet for many wedding suppliers, who may be more willing to consider giving a discount in order to secure your business at these times than in the busy summer months.

Q *If I have to cancel the wedding, where do I stand financially with suppliers?*

A In this situation you will be in breach of contract and will usually forfeit any deposit paid. You may also have to pay compensation to, say, a caterer for any financial loss suffered as a result of your breach of contract. This would normally amount to any profit element the firm loses on your deal. However, the caterer does have a responsibility to keep losses to a minimum. The more notice you can give of cancellation, the better the chance that suppliers' losses will be small. If you pull out at the last moment, they will be unlikely to get another booking, and your liability may be greater. (See Chapter 21 for information on insurance.)

VAT

VAT currently stands at 17.5 per cent, but suppliers with an annual turnover of less than £54,000 are not usually VAT-registered, and not all goods are subject to VAT. However, most items associated with weddings attract VAT, with a few exceptions.

- **children's clothing** A child is defined as being under the age of 14, and the zero-rated clothes are only those that fit a child of 13 years or less (height 158cm, chest 84cm, waist 71cm, hips 86cm and shoe size 1½). However, if you have outfits specially made for your child attendants and you provide the dressmaker with the material you will have to pay VAT on the material. You will have to pay VAT on the dressmaker's time only if he or she is VAT-registered

- **wedding cakes** (if they are supplied independently of other catering)
- **food provided by the caterer that requires further preparation by the customer** (such as defrosting, cooking, re-heating or arranging or serving on plates) is not subject to VAT.

Look at estimates or quotations you receive to see if VAT is included or ask the supplier if there is VAT to pay. If there is, that particular supplier is VAT-registered, and you may be able to make savings by looking for one who is not.

Budget breakdown

The table overleaf shows how the average total cost of £13,000 for a traditional white wedding is made up. The cost of some of these items could be up to 20 per cent higher if you are getting married in London.

In reality, many couples spend somewhere near the average for the majority of their costs, make savings where they can or where the item does not feature on their list of priorities, and spending more where something – the reception meal, say, or the honeymoon destination – is particularly important to them.

What is not included
These figures do not include the cost of any other celebration, such as an engagement party or stag and hen nights. Miscellaneous costs, such as cash spent on the day and so on are not included.

What it costs: the hard facts

Below are more details on the amounts given in the table overleaf, plus some cost-cutting suggestions.

Church/register office/approved premises fees

The fee for the publication of banns is £15, the marriage service costs £142, and the marriage certificate £3.50. Church fees usually mount up to about £260, which includes the additional cost of the organist, church choir, bells and heating.

Item	£
Church fees	260
Bride's wedding clothes	900
Bride's going-away outfit	200
Bride's beauty treatments	80
Attendants' outfits	500
Groom's wedding outfit	250
Engagement ring	850
Bride's wedding ring	200
Groom's wedding ring	150
Transport	500
Photographs	500
Video	450
Flowers	350
Reception	
Hire of venue	750
Catering/food	2,500
Drink	900
Cake	250
Entertainment	700
Wedding stationery	200
Insurance	60
First night hotel	150
Honeymoon	2,300
Total	**13,000**

For a civil service at a register office, the cheapest possible wedding is £97.50, which includes £30 per person for the superintendent registrar's certificates, a fee of £34 for the registrar's attendance on the day of the wedding, and £3.50 for a copy of your marriage certificate, issued on the day of the wedding. For a wedding on approved premises, the superintendent registrar's certificates again cost £30 per person. In addition you will have to pay a fee set by the

Budget checklist

Item	Estimated cost	Actual cost	Who pays?	Deposit	Paid	Balance £
Press announcements						
Engagement						
Wedding						
Engagement party						
Wedding venue fees						
Bride						
Dress						
Veil or hat						
Shoes						
Lingerie/tights/stockings						
Jewellery						
Going-away outfit						
Beauty treatments						
Make-up						
Hairdresser						

Item	Estimated cost	Actual cost	Who pays?	Deposit	Paid	Balance £
Groom						
Wedding clothes						
Going-away outfit						
Barber						
Bridesmaids						
Adults' dresses						
Adults' headdresses						
Adults' shoes						
Children's dresses						
Children's headdresses						
Children's shoes						
Pages						
Outfits						
Shoes						
Ushers' outfits						

Best man's outfit

Bride's father's outfit

Rings

Engagement ring

Bride's wedding ring

Groom's wedding ring

Transport

Bride and father to ceremony

Bride's mother and attendants to ceremony

Groom and best man to ceremony

Bride and groom to reception

Attendants and bride's parents to reception

Bride and groom from reception

Photographs

Item	Estimated cost	Actual cost	Who pays?	Deposit	Paid	Balance £
Video						
Flowers						
Bride's bouquet						
Bride's headdress						
Bridesmaids' bouquets						
Bridesmaids' headdresses						
Buttonholes and corsages						
Wedding venue decorations						
Car decorations						
Reception decorations						
Reception						
Hire of venue						
Other hire costs (staff, furniture, crockery etc.)						
Food						
Drink						
Crèche service						
Entertainment						

Service charge/tips							
Other							
Honeymoon							
First night hotel							
Holiday							
Spending money							
Stationery							
Invitations							
Postage							
Order of service sheets							
Menus							
Place cards							
Other reception stationery							
Wedding insurance							
Hen and stag nights							
Any other costs							
Contingency of 5–10%							

local authority for the superintendent registrar and registrar to attend the ceremony, and will also have to pay any charge made for the use of the premises.

Bride's clothes

The average cost of a traditional wedding dress with veil, headdress and shoes is £900. If you want to spend less than this, you could hire a dress for about £300. Another option would be to make your own (which can be cheaper as long as the pattern doesn't require a large amount of expensive material) – see pages 102–3. A secondhand dress could cost under £100, or you could borrow one from a friend or relative, which will cost nothing at all.

The average amount a bride spends on a going-away outfit is £200, but you could wear a dress or suit you already have if you prefer.

Bride's beauty treatments, make-up, hair

A budget of about £80 would cover some new cosmetics, a manicure and a session with the hairdresser on the day, although you could use your existing cosmetics and get friends to give you a manicure and do your hair.

Attendants' outfits

The average total cost is in the region of £500, but this clearly depends on the number of attendants you have. If you don't want to splash out and have the attendants' outfits specially made, you could look in high-street stores for inexpensive outfits. Other options are to make them yourself or look for secondhand ones.

Groom's wedding clothes

Hiring full morning dress costs about £60 and buying a suit off-the-peg costs between £150 and £300. Do not forget to allow for shirt, tie and shoes. Alternatively, you could wear an existing suit or borrow one from a friend.

Rings

The average cost of an engagement ring is £850, and £200 for the bride's wedding ring. The groom's wedding ring generally costs about £150. If you want to spend less than this on an engagement ring, shop around for less expensive designs and look for semi-precious stones or smaller diamonds. Alternatively, you could wear a family ring if you have one.

Transport

Expect to pay £400-plus for cars (two cars for about three hours), although if you want to save money, you could use cars belonging to family or friends.

Photographs/video

Using a professional photographer for the day will cost about £500. To bring this cost down to about £200, you could have a simple, civil ceremony and go for the minimum number of shots. A professional video of the day, starting with the bride's departure from her house and ending after the speeches at the reception, will cost about £450. A shorter video, ending after the ceremony, costs £300 or less. Alternatively, you could get friends and relatives to take photographs/video for you, as long as you are confident of their abilities. Work out a list of important photographs and make one person responsible for taking them so that no vital moment or person is left out.

Flowers

On average, couples spend £250 to £350 on flowers for the day.

- A fairly simple, hand-tied bouquet costs £50-plus, while a wired shower style starts at about £100.
- Fresh flower headdresses cost from £35.
- Buttonholes are around £3.50 each (for a carnation), corsages £7.50 to £10.
- Floral arrangements for the church could cost from £100 and decorations for the reception range from £150, although costs vary quite dramatically depending on where in the UK you live.

However, flowers do not need to cost this much, and a skilled friend or relation could arrange the flowers for much less. If another couple is marrying on the same day you may be able to share the cost of flowers at the church, or you could choose to use the flowers that the church provides. If you pay for flowers in the church, check whether you can take some of them to the reception venue. Flowers in season and simple arrangements cost less than hot-house blooms lavishly displayed and can be just as effective.

The reception

The number of guests is the crucial factor here, with 100 being the average.

- The average cost of hiring a venue to accommodate this number is £750.
- Catering adds another £2,500 to the bill.
- Allow £900 for drinks.
- The wedding cake costs about £250.
- Entertainment: as a guide, a band playing for 3 hours costs from £500.
- A DJ playing recorded music for 3 hours would cost from £300.
- A string quartet playing background music for 3 hours would cost about £600.

Ways of cutting the cost for the reception include:

- holding the reception at home, or in a hall, which is cheaper than a hotel
- having a finger buffet instead of a sit-down meal
- offering sparkling wine rather than real champagne
- making the cake yourself, getting a friend to make it (this can cost nearly half the amount of having one professionally made) or buying one ready-made from a supermarket and having the icing done professionally
- having a short reception, which does not go on into the evening, saves on the cost of entertainment and refreshments
- having a paying bar instead of providing all the alcohol yourselves, or providing drinks for part of the evening, then having a paying bar.

Wedding stationery

The average total cost of stationery is about £200, including invitations, order of service sheets and reception items (place setting cards). It is cheaper to buy invitations ready-printed from stationers and fill in your own details or create your own on a computer (see pages 69–70). Also, you do not need to have service sheets (you can use the church's service and hymn books), menus etc.

Wedding insurance

Comprehensive cover can cost between £50 and £300 – see Chapter 21, page 205. However, you may decide to take the risk and save the money, particularly if you are having a small, simple wedding.

First night and honeymoon

The average cost of a hotel for the first night is £150. An increasing number of couples have a two-week honeymoon abroad, which costs on average £2,300. You can save money if you spend your first night at home or at a simple country inn or hotel. Choosing a shorter stay in the UK will keep the cost down. Renting a cottage is a cheaper option, particularly out of season, but make sure it is comfortable and well heated. Spending a few nights in France, Italy or Spain, for example, costs less than flying to a distant destination.

A couple who made money on their reception

Debbie and Adam were on a very tight budget. After a family register office ceremony, they asked 50 guests to a lunchtime buffet followed by square dancing. Both wore clothes they already owned for the ceremony, while Debbie found a wedding dress in a charity shop for £35 so she could look the part at the reception. As they had been living together for a couple of years they did not want household gifts, so instead asked everyone to contribute food or drink for the reception. They ended up with plenty of food. One aunt provided a whole dressed salmon, the groom's father gave a case of champagne, and puddings and salads were plentiful. What they had not expected was that some guests would give gifts of money instead of, or in addition to, food and drink. These more than covered the hire of the hall, band, photographer, glasses and crockery and other incidental expenses, and they finished with about £50 in hand.

Chapter 5

Financing your wedding

Getting married is not just a major personal pledge, it also represents an enormous financial commitment. While a no-frills register office do (excluding entertaining your guests afterwards) costs just under £100, according to *www.confetti.co.uk* – a website devoted to all things wedding-related – the average cost of a traditional white wedding (including honeymoon) is about £13,000. It is estimated that in seven years' time, the cost of the average white wedding will have risen to £20,000 – largely because in recent years, the cost of weddings has risen by more than twice the rate of general inflation.

Although you won't have to pay for the cost of your wedding all in one go, you will need to have money available to pay deposits for wedding services – such as the reception venue, catering, wedding dress and photographs – as soon as you book them. Before you start spending, however, it is essential to have a reasonable idea of the total cost by drawing up a detailed budget – see Chapter 4. This will give you an idea of how much money you have to pay upfront and will also help you decide how you are going to finance your wedding. This can be with savings, by borrowing or by using a combination of the two.

Saving for wedding costs

The cheapest way to pay for your wedding is with savings you already have. However, if you have no savings – or the amount you have saved is not enough – meeting the cost out of savings may not be an option. How you choose to finance it will depend on how much spare cash you have, how far in advance you have begun planning and how much your wedding is going to cost. The Table below shows the approximate amount you would need to save each month to pay for a range of wedding costs and time periods.

How much you need to save

	Monthly saving required if your wedding will cost:			
Time available to save	**£5,000**	**£10,000**	**£15,000**	**£20,000**
6 months	£800	£1,700	£2,500	£3,300
12 months	£400	£800	£1,250	£1,700
18 months	£300	£600	£800	£1,100
24 months	£200	£400	£600	£800

Figures have been rounded to the nearest 100.

Even if saving the full amount looks impossible, it would be worth saving as much as you can in the months leading up to the wedding. If you have not yet set a date, you could consider post-poning it for a few months so – for example – you can at least save up enough to pay all the deposits.

Two properties?

If both you and your partner each own property, it could be worth moving in together before the wedding and selling one of them. Not only could you use some of the cash raised from the sale to put towards your wedding but you could also save the monthly amount that was going towards the mortgage. If it's not a good time to sell, an alternative would be to let one of your properties out.

Paying for your wedding with a loan

If you do not have any savings – or you don't have enough to meet the whole cost – you could look at ways of reducing what you plan to spend on your wedding or you could take out a loan. However, you should be aware that, because of the interest you have to pay on the loan, borrowing will push up the cost of your wedding quite considerably.

And before taking the loan route, consider how you will feel in a few years' time when you will still be paying for the wedding. Then think hard about the sorts of financial commitments you are likely to have in the future. For example, are you likely to have children? Will you want to move to a bigger home and so be paying a large amount towards your mortgage?

If you think your financial commitments are likely to be onerous within several years, try to borrow as little as possible and try to repay the loan over as short a time as possible.

The main ways of borrowing are set out below but however you decide to borrow, the most important thing to consider is how much you can afford to repay each month. This is because the consequences of not repaying a loan can result in your being taken to court and getting a bad credit record. Working out how much you can afford to repay also tells you how quickly you can pay off the loan: the longer it takes, the higher the total cost of the loan because there's more interest to pay.

Paying for your honeymoon

It is a good idea to pay for your honeymoon with a credit card because of the extra protection you get from the Consumer Credit Act. If you have a problem with anything you pay for by credit card (between £100 and £30,000) and your supplier won't help, you can seek compensation from your credit-card issuer. For example, if your honeymoon is a disaster because your hotel was a building site and you cannot get redress from the tour operator, you can claim the money from your credit-card company. You are often charged a fee for paying for the whole of your holiday by credit card, so to avoid this you could pay the deposit for it (minimum of £100) by credit card and the rest with cash (if possible). If you do this you will still be covered by the Consumer Credit Act.

Which type of loan?

Given the sums involved, it is unlikely that an overdraft on your current account is going to be sufficient – and given that your bank can demand that you repay an overdraft at any time, it's not a very practical option either.

Credit cards

Unless you have a sufficiently high credit limit on your credit card, it is unlikely to be suitable for meeting the whole cost of your wedding. However, using a credit card for part of the cost could be worth considering but only if you have a card with a low interest rate (you can get details of low-rate cards by checking the personal finance pages of the weekend press). You could also take out a card specifically for wedding-related purchases which could provide a convenient way of keeping an eye on your budget.

Personal loans

A popular way of borrowing to pay for a wedding is to take out a personal loan – these are available from banks, building societies and other lenders. The virtue of a personal loan is convenience coupled with certainty. Based on how much you can afford to repay each month, you decide how much you want to borrow and for how long. Repayments are then fixed for the duration of the loan so you know exactly how much you need to repay each month – see the Table below for typical costs.

Typical cost of an unsecured personal loan

Size of loan	\\multicolumn{5}{l}{Monthly cost of a loan repaid over:}
	1 year	2 years	3 years	4 years	5 years
Without payment protection insurance					
£5,000	£440	£230	£160	£120	£100
£10,000	£870	£450	£320	£250	£200
£15,000	£1,300	£680	£470	£370	£310
£20,000	£1,740	£910	£630	£490	£410
With payment protection insurance					
£5,000	£470	£250	£180	£140	£120
£10,000	£930	£500	£350	£290	£240
£15,000	£1,400	£750	£530	£430	£360
£20,000	£1,860	£1,000	£700	£570	£480

Figures have been rounded to the nearest £10 and are correct at November 2001.

When comparing the cost of personal loans, always make sure that you are comparing like with like: a loan repaid over two years is always going to look more expensive (in monthly terms), than a loan repaid over three years.

Another thing to watch out for with a personal loan is the extra cost of loan payment protection insurance which many lenders try to sell alongside the loan. This kind of insurance – which aims to pay out if you're not earning because of ill-health or unemployment – is usually quite restrictive and it can push up the price of borrowing quite considerably. However, it's easy not to notice this – a common ploy in personal loan literature is to make the repayments with insurance look far more attractive than those without it or to print the rates without insurance in tiny hard-to-read type.

Tip

Don't automatically assume that your bank is the best place to get a loan. Rates vary tremendously and high-street banks rarely have the best deals. Other lenders – Internet banks especially – often offer much more competitive rates. You can get details by checking the personal finance pages in the national press.

Secured personal loans

Most personal loans are unsecured although you can get personal loans which are secured on your property. Secured personal loans tend to be cheaper than their unsecured counterpart but the risk is that if you fail to keep up repayments, you could lose your home.

Increasing your mortgage

In terms of the monthly cost, a reasonably cheap way of financing a lump sum is to increase your mortgage (another type of secured loan) – provided your lender will let you. Even using the typical rate of 6 per cent charged by most high-street lenders (in November 2001), borrowing £13,000 would add about £65 to your monthly outgoings. However, this option is expensive in terms of the total interest charged. And – as with secured personal loans – if you don't keep up your mortgage repayments, you risk losing your home.

A loan from your insurer

If you have an endowment policy (a type of insurance-based savings plan), you may be able to borrow money against the current value of the policy. Your insurer will be able to tell you whether this is a possibility, and also what your expected monthly repayments would be so that you can compare them with other forms of borrowing.

'I did babysitting jobs to help pay for my daughter's wedding'

Barbara and Graham's daughter and her fiancé had set their hearts on a large white wedding, with a reception for over 100 guests at an Elizabethan manor country hotel. The estimated cost was between £10,000 and £12,000. The couple was able to contribute £4,000, and Barbara and Graham agreed to pay the rest.

'We had about £3,000 in savings and decided to take out a bank loan for £5,000 over two years. The repayments worked out at about £250 a month. So the only problem was where to get the money to repay the loan. A colleague then told me that she had been babysitting for a number of families and that there was plenty of work in the area. This struck me as a good way to earn some of the money to repay the loan and I was able to charge £5 per hour.

'It wasn't long before I was babysitting regularly and earning up to £80 per week. In the weeks leading up to Christmas and at New Year I was working every evening and once or twice stayed the night so that the parents could stay out longer.

'I babysat for about 18 months and earned £4,500. After that I worked less often and eventually stopped altogether once I had earned all the money I needed.'

Chapter 6

Planning ahead

All weddings, whether large or small, require meticulous planning. You will need to make lots of lists and keep an assiduous check on what has been done and what remains to be done. Book your key venues and suppliers as early as you can – you can think about the details later. Do not feel that you have to take care of every last item yourself and delegate wherever you can. In this chapter is a detailed list of what you should be doing when.

Wedding organisers

If you just don't have the time to make all the arrangements yourself, and there is no one in the family who can take on the job, you could consider using a professional wedding organiser. This option is currently chosen by only about one per cent of UK couples, but the industry is growing fast, as couples realise that using an organiser can both ease the burden of endless decision-making, and save them time.

Experienced wedding organisers are excellent managers and negotiators, and are very knowledgeable about where to get the best deals on services and supplies. They may be able to negotiate discounts that individuals could not achieve. You can use a wedding organiser to take over as much or as little of the arrangements as you like. Part of the organiser's job is to discuss with you exactly what you want and to refer back to you before making any final arrangements, so that you remain in control.

What a wedding organiser can do

- Deal with the legalities of a civil wedding.
- Help you personalise your ceremony.
- Keep a tight grip on your outgoings. You agree a budget with the organiser at the outset, and he or she organises the wedding within those constraints. The organiser must provide you with a breakdown of costs, check contracts and monitor deposits and when payments are due.
- Recommend services and suppliers, such as photographer, florist, entertainers, and, if you wish, make all the arrangements with them, including negotiating prices.
- Send out invitations and monitor replies.
- Oversee and co-ordinate all arrangements, both before the wedding and on the day.
- You can also ask an organiser to deal with just one aspect of the day, such as finding a venue that fits with your particular requirements. A nominal fee of around £50–£75 would usually be charged for this.

To find a wedding organiser, first ask around your friends and colleagues for word-of-mouth recommendations, or look in the classified sections of wedding magazines, or search wedding websites (see Addresses). Some approved licensed premises have an 'in-house' wedding organiser, who can co-ordinate the arrangements. Overseas tour operators may also have specialist staff who can oversee a wedding that is taking place abroad.

Before you sign any contract with an organiser, read the small print and make sure you know exactly what the terms are. Some charge a flat fee, often around £1,000, while others take 10–15 per cent of the total cost, which would work out far more expensive if you are having a large wedding. Before you book, follow up a couple of references from previous clients and get a detailed written quotation, outlining exactly what the organiser will and will not do.

Soon after your engagement

- Decide what type of wedding you are going to have: religious or civil, formal or informal.

- Draw up your preliminary budget (see Chapter 4).
- Decide who will pay for what.
- Work out how many guests you can afford/want to invite and draw up a guest list.
- Choose and book location for ceremony (you can book up to a year ahead for a civil ceremony, and may be able to make a provisional booking even further ahead).
- Cut out snippets from magazines and newspapers and surf the Internet (see Addresses) for ideas on flowers, dresses etc. (and keep a wedding file). Start a wedding notebook and carry it with you. Use it to jot down ideas and note names, numbers, estimates, dates and so on.
- Find out if you need to make any special arrangements regarding a wedding licence (see the Appendix), and if so start the necessary procedures.
- Choose and book venue for reception. Be sure to get a written confirmation.
- Approach best man and attendants and make sure they keep the date free.
- Book the following and get written confirmations for:
  photographer
  video operator
  florist
  transport
  caterers
  toastmaster (if you are having one)
  entertainment for the reception.
- Order the wedding cake.
- Book the honeymoon.
- Book the wedding abroad (if having one).
- (Bride) shop for dresses and accessories for self and bridesmaids and place orders if these are being made for you.
- Start working out the details of the reception.

Allow plenty of time to make all your wedding arrangements, particularly if you are both working, or if you are not already living together and thus have less opportunity to discuss things. If you are getting married away from where you live – at your parents' home town, for instance – you will need to schedule in several visits to the venue to organise all the local services such as transport, flowers and caterers. You will also need to spend time in the evenings and at weekends on organisation.

Setting the date and time

- For a formal wedding allow a bare minimum of three months for the organisation. Six is better, and a year is not too long if you want to marry at a popular venue on a Saturday. Some churches and reception venues are booked up for many months in advance, especially for summer weddings.
- Compare diaries early on to make sure you avoid other commitments and ensure all the key guests are free on the date you have chosen.
- Church weddings are not usually allowed on Sundays. Saturday is the most popular day, although there is nothing to stop you choosing a weekday if the minister agrees.
- By law, in England and Wales, a wedding must take place between 8am and 6pm, although Quaker and Jewish weddings, are exceptions to this rule. In Scotland a religious wedding can take place at any time as long as the minister agrees.
- A civil wedding at a register office must take place during the hours when the office is open, usually Monday to Friday, 9am to 4pm and Saturday mornings from 9am until 1pm. Approved licensed premises are likely to be more flexible over timings, and can be booked for a whole day and evening, if the reception is taking place at the same venue. It may also be possible to get married on a Sunday or public holiday at approved licensed premises, as long as you can persuade the superintendent registrar and registrar to attend, and can organise the other suppliers and services you need.
- Some Christian ministers prefer not to conduct weddings during Lent (the period leading up to Easter). If you are permitted to marry at this time, you may not be allowed to decorate the church with flowers.
- If you marry on a winter's afternoon, the light outdoors may not be very good for photographs. Winter weather may also be a limiting factor if guests have to travel far.

Four to six months to go

- Order the wedding invitations (printing takes two to four weeks). Some couples send out invitations at this stage, so that people can make sure their holiday arrangements or other commitments don't clash with the wedding date. For a big wedding, sending invitations early leaves you time to send out a second round of invitations if many people refuse.
- Draw up a wedding gift list (or organise one at a department store – see pages 93–5).
- If making your own fruit cake, bake it now.
- Contact the minister to confirm dates of the banns and details of the wedding.
- Book bellringers.
- Decide on the form of service and hymns you want for a church wedding.
- Arrange to meet organist and choir master to discuss choice of music, and book organist and choir or soloist.
- Book hotel for wedding night.
- Decide what the men in the wedding party will wear and buy any clothes needed.
- Consider arranging wedding insurance (see Chapter 21).
- Set up your own website, if having one (see pages 70–1).

Two to three months to go

- Arrange a rehearsal for the ceremony.
- Check passports; apply for new or amended ones if necessary (see pages 65–6).
- Apply for any visas needed for your honeymoon.
- Send out invitations, six to nine weeks before the wedding, if you have not already done so.
- Check off replies as they arrive.
- Book overnight accommodation for any guests who need it.
- Send gift list to those who request it.
- Make a list of the gifts (and who they are from) as they arrive and write thank-you letters immediately.
- Meet caterers to agree food and drink menus.

- Buy wedding ring(s).
- Buy wedding gifts for each other.
- Buy gifts for best man and attendants.
- Book groom's, best man's and ushers' morning suits if hiring (allow six weeks).
- Buy your wedding shoes and underwear before your first dress fitting so you can try on the whole ensemble together. Wear the shoes around the house so they are comfortable on the day.
- Have first wedding dress fitting.
- Shop for going-away outfit.
- Shop for honeymoon clothes.
- Take your headdress along to the hairdresser to discuss a suitable style and have a trial run if necessary. Make an appointment for the day.
- Have a session with a beautician and try out any different make-up well in advance of the day. Make an appointment for the day.
- Book any beauty treatments you will want to have before the wedding.
- Have any vaccinations needed for the honeymoon. Some can make you feel unwell, so choose a time when you can rest if necessary.
- Visit family planning clinic if necessary (see overleaf).
- Decide on bouquets, buttonholes, corsages and floral arrangements needed for church and reception and order them.
- Order other stationery such as order of service sheets and items for the reception or design your own on a computer (see pages 69–70).

One month to go

- Check that any guests who have failed to reply did receive their invitations.
- Draw up a draft seating plan if you are having a sit-down meal.
- Confirm date of wedding rehearsal.
- Hear banns read in church.
- Arrange for photographer to visit venue with you to prepare a list of specific shots.
- Prepare a newspaper announcement.
- (Bride) book manicure for the day before.

Your period needn't spoil your day

If your periods are very regular, either naturally or because you take the combined pill, five minutes spent with your diary will reveal whether a period is due on or around your wedding day or honeymoon. If this is likely to cause you a problem, talk to your GP or family planning clinic at least a month before the wedding day for advice on how you can use the combined pill to alter the dates on which your period will arrive. If you are not taking the pill, or use the progestogen-only pill, you could consider taking the combined pill for the short term in order to benefit in this way, but should take medical advice beforehand, as the combined pill is not suitable for all women.

If you have never taken the pill before, you should visit the clinic two to three months before your wedding, so that you have time to get over any of the minor side-effects which women often experience when they start the pill.

Alternatively, a doctor or nurse can prescribe other hormonal tablets which delay the onset of a period, without having any contraceptive effect. If you are going to a long-haul destination for your honeymoon be aware of the effect that passing through different time zones will have on when you should take your pill. Again, see your GP or clinic in advance for advice. The Family Planning Association Helpline* can give advice on these and other matters.

- Check that everyone in the wedding party has their correct wedding attire.
- (Bride) have final fitting for wedding dress. Leave this fitting as late as possible, since many brides lose weight before the wedding.
- Advise bank etc. of change of address and name (see overleaf).
- Arrange stag night and hen party.
- If you feel stressed over the next few weeks, give yourself a day off from thinking about the wedding, or try some pleasant distraction such as a long walk, a massage, or a comedy show.

> **Tip**
>
> Leave it as late as possible to finalise your seating plan and allow for some flexibility. People may cancel or decide that they can come after all just days before the event.

Two weeks to go

- Write and practise speeches.
- Ice and decorate the cake if making it yourself.
- Order traveller's cheques or currency for honeymoon.
- Confirm all the arrangements: florist, photographer, video operator, cars, reception, cake, church details and honeymoon.
- Have stag night and hen party.

One week to go

- Wrap gifts for attendants, best man and each other.
- (Groom) place correct fees for minister, organist, choir, bell-ringers and church heating in cash in marked envelopes and give to best man, together with keys for going-away car on the day.
- Time the journey to the church so you know exactly what time you will need to leave home.
- Pack honeymoon luggage and check travel details and tickets. You can finish packing the night before the wedding if necessary.
- Have wedding rehearsal.
- Arrange for someone to take care of bride's dress and accessories after the wedding (usually her mother). The best man should take charge of the groom's clothes and, if they are hired, return them.
- Review the seating plan and prepare place cards.
- Confirm final number of guests to caterer.
- Think through the logistics of the whole day: who is doing what, when and where. Doing this will help you identify any last-minute arrangements that are needed.

The day before

- If using your own car to go on your honeymoon, check that it has petrol, oil and water and is in perfect running order.
- Pack going-away/honeymoon clothes and if possible have case(s) taken to reception venue.
- Give the best man and attendants their presents.
- (Bride) have manicure.
- Double-check all the arrangements.

Changing your surname

Every woman who marries has to decide whether or not to change her surname. You are not legally obliged to do so. The various options are listed below.

- **Changing to husband's surname** This is easy and makes any joint ventures straightforward. To make the change, send a copy of your marriage certificate to the relevant organisations (banks and building societies will want to see the original), so that they can change their records.
- Another common choice is to **keep your maiden name for work purposes**, using the title Miss or Ms as you prefer, and use your married name and the title Mrs elsewhere. Think this through before you make any changes, as confusion can easily set in if you are not consistent. If your job involves a lot of travel tell your employer if you change your passport and bank details.
- See page 31 if you have children from a previous marriage or relationship.
- You could use **both your surnames, hyphenated** if you wish. If both of you decide to adopt a new composite surname, you will need to change your names by deed poll or by statutory declaration after your marriage. A solicitor can advise on how to do this.
- Your **husband could change his surname to your maiden name**. However, unlike women, men do not have a legal right to change their name on marriage, so he would need to make the change by deed poll or statutory declaration.

- If you do choose to change your surname you should inform:
  your employer
  Inland Revenue★
  the Contributions Agency★ and the Benefits Agency★ (both part of the Department of Social Security – DSS)
  bank
  building society
  insurance companies
  credit-card and store-card companies
  passport office (see below)
  legal adviser
  financial adviser
  pension providers (if you have a personal pension or contribute to an FSAVC – free-standing additional voluntary contribution scheme)
  DVLA★ (the Driver and Vehicle Licensing Agency) to change driver's licence and vehicle registration documents
  Premium Bonds Office★
  any companies of which you are a shareholder
  motoring organisations
  any professional associations to which you belong
  any other clubs or societies
  GP
  dentist.

If you are on the Internet, you may wish to change your email address.

Travel documents for your honeymoon and changing your passport

- If you are going abroad on honeymoon and wish to **travel using your married name** you can change your passport up to three months before the wedding. You can do this either by surrendering your existing passport with no refund for unexpired time, and applying for a new standard ten-year passport; or by having your current passport updated. Either way, the changed passport cannot be used until the date of your marriage.
- Whether you opt for a completely new passport, costing £28, or an amended one, costing £17, you will need to send a standard

Application Form and a copy of Form PD2, completed by the person who will be conducting the ceremony. These forms are available from most post offices and from regional passport offices,★ or you can download an Application Form (but not Form PD2) from the website of the UK Passport Service. Further information is available on the website (*www.ukpa.gov.uk*), or you can ring the helpline (see Addresses).

- **Allow at least one month for the application to be processed** and up to three months if applying between February and June. If you leave it late, you can visit the London Passport Office★ in person and apply for a new passport or have one amended on the spot. Be prepared for a long wait if you visit at a busy time of year.

- **Check that the name on your passport and visa is the same as the name on your travel documents**. You can travel using your maiden name and change your passport on your return; or if the tickets are in your married name, take your marriage certificate with your existing passport. However, some countries will not grant a visa on post-dated or amended passports, nor on a passport in your maiden name accompanied by a marriage certificate. Check with the relevant consulate in advance. If you do change your name on your passport, remember to inform your tour operator as some assume you will be travelling under your maiden name. It is frustrating to go to the trouble of changing your passport only to find you have to take your marriage certificate after all because your tickets are in your maiden name.

On the day

In the hours before the ceremony:
Timings given are for a traditional church wedding. Timings for civil weddings are given on pages 148 and 151.

- the bride has her hair done, does her make-up and dresses
- flowers arrive at bride's home
- bridesmaids arrive and change
- chief bridesmaid or bride's mother helps bride arrange her veil
- best man and groom dress in their wedding clothes
- best man checks that he has the rings

- groom gives best man any cash or cheques he may need to pay for church facilities etc. plus any travel documents etc. for the honeymoon
- going-away clothes are taken to reception venue
- going-away/honeymoon luggage taken to reception venue
- groom's car left at reception venue if it is to be used to leave the reception
- best man collects buttonholes and order of service sheets to take to church.

Shortly before the ceremony:

- ushers arrive at church 45 minutes before ceremony begins
- couple and guests arrive at register office about 10 minutes before the service is due to begin
- photographer and video operator arrive at wedding venue
- organist arrives at church and begins to play quietly about half an hour before the ceremony is due to begin
- minister, choir and bellringers arrive about half an hour before the service begins.
- guests begin to arrive at the church and are given order of service sheets by ushers, who also direct them to their places according to the plan (see page 159)
- best man and groom arrive at the church about 40 minutes before the ceremony begins and pose for photographs, then take their positions in the front pew on the right of the aisle. Best man may pay the minister now or after the service
- bridesmaids and bride's mother leave for church and pose for photographs on arrival, about 10 minutes before the ceremony
- bride's mother is escorted to her place in the front pew to the left of the aisle. She leaves a seat on her right for the bride's father
- bride and her father leave for church and are met in church porch by bridesmaids. They pose for photographs. Chief bridesmaid arranges bride's dress, train and veil. Ushers take their seats in church. The minister greets the bride at the church door and can then either precede her down the aisle or return to the chancel steps and wait for her there. The choir can either head the procession or be already seated in the choir stalls.

Chapter 7

Using a computer to enhance your wedding

Gathering wedding information from the Internet can save you time and energy, as can putting your wedding information on to your own website. If you have access to a computer and printer, you can use them to create your own wedding stationery, and to keep up-to-date records of all your wedding plans. You can also use digital photography to view, edit and print wedding pictures using your computer.

Wedding websites

There are numerous websites dedicated to helping you plan your wedding. A selection is included in Addresses (page 236), but there are dozens, if not hundreds, more.

The content and quality of websites varies widely. Many sites emanate from the USA, and are of limited use to British couples, so look for the suffix *.co.uk* in the website address, or browse round the site looking for a UK contact address.

Browsing round the web can provide you with lots of ideas, and save valuable time in the hunt for suppliers and services. Among the types of sites you can expect to find are:

- General information sites, offering planning advice, etiquette pointers, ideas for dresses etc. Many of these will also have links to suppliers. They may also have 'chat rooms', where you can exchange ideas with other couples via typed messages, or just browse through what other people have to say.

- Directory sites, listing suppliers by type and area, with links to suppliers' websites, plus other contact details. There are also sites listing details of wedding venues.
- Specialised sites, concentrating on just one aspect such as wedding gift suppliers, or wedding organisers, who will do some or all of the planning for you (see page 56).
- Sites which help you to create your own website and offer downloadable software.
- Local register offices may have their own site with details of the venues and ceremonies on offer.

As well as going to specialised wedding sites, you can use the web to search for poetry and readings, ideas for music, honeymoon destinations and so on. You can even get speeches. For some pointers, check out *www.thebestman.com*, or look at *www.hitched.co.uk* or *www.usabride.com/wedplan/a_bestman_speech.html*. Alternatively you can search at *www.google.co.uk* under 'best man speech'.

Wedding software

If you enjoy using a computer, and have access to a printer, you could consider producing your own wedding stationery. Specially designed wedding software provides the templates and decorative images needed to create invitations, orders of service, menus, place cards and so on. To get the best results, print on good-quality paper, at the highest specification available on your printer. Some stationers such as W H Smith and Staples stock packs of ready-made blanks of invitations and menu stationery, which you can customise for wedding use by printing on your own information.

Some software packages are designed only to create stationery, while others also have a planning element. Features vary, but you might find:

- budget planner, to track spending
- wedding gift list
- guest list
- seating planner
- some packages also include a picture-editing tool which you can use to play about with wedding photographs. To do this you

would either need to take photographs with a digital camera and download them directly to your computer, or else, when you have a conventional film developed, ask the photo processor to put the images on to a Kodak 'Flashpix' CD, as well as producing prints. If you have a scanner you can scan in your photos.

Wedding software packages are available from retailers but you will also find a wide selection available for downloading – sometimes free – from the web. See Addresses, or try searching 'wedding software' on *www.google.co.uk* for a selection. Many packages are made in the USA so may need to be adapted for British use.

If you are already a dab hand at using your computer, you may not need specialised software at all. Most computers have a wide range of fonts and decorative effects already installed, as part of either a word-processing or desk-top publishing package. With a scanner and some picture-editing software you can add photographs or illustrations of your choice. You can also use an existing database program to create guest lists etc.

Your own wedding website

An increasing number of couples set up a wedding website for friends and relatives to visit both before and after the wedding.

What to put on your site
There are all sorts of features you can include on your website, some of which are purely for fun, while others are very practical.

- Pictures of yourselves as children, engagement pictures, the story of how you met, and how you got engaged.
- Date and time of the wedding.
- Details of how to find the wedding/reception venues, with downloadable maps for guests to print out.
- Information on local B&Bs and hotels, for guests who will need overnight accommodation.
- 'Cast list' of all the principal participants.
- Guest list.
- Wedding gift list. Guests can consult the list then contact the store separately.

- Chat room where guests can ask questions or make comments. This is complicated to set up yourself, but you can create your own chat room on Yahoo!.
- After the wedding, you can post pictures of the day itself.

How to create a website

Mid-price web design programs such as FrontPage are simple to use, and you don't need to be an expert to get good results. First, you'll need some free web space, usually available from your Internet service provider. Most web design programs provide templates where you fill in the text and pictures you want to use. If you want to be more creative, you can design your own pages. Once the site is as you want it, you will probably need a File Transfer Protocol (FTP) file manager program, which you can download from the Internet. The total cost of producing a website like this is around £150. For more details on suitable software, see the Appendix.

Naming your web site is important. You will need to think of an Internet address that no one else has taken (*www.ourwedding.com* had been taken, for instance, but *www.johnlovesalice.com* was still available at the time of writing). Then you need to go to a domain name registrar and register it. This is fairly simple – you just put your chosen name in the search facility to check that it hasn't been taken, and give your credit-card details to buy it for one or two years – this will cost up to £50, depending on your choice of registrar. Two examples are uk2.net and freeserve-v1.domainnames.com.

Once you have registered the name, you can either use the same service to store your web pages (which will cost more), or you can put your website up on some free space, and set things up so anyone typing your registered name is automatically diverted there. The registrar will be able to explain your options.

Digital photography

Digital cameras are becoming increasingly popular and can now produce pictures of a quality comparable to those taken with film cameras.

- Digital cameras do not use film, but store images digitally which can be downloaded on to a computer, then transferred to floppy disk or CD-Rom. There are no processing costs, so you save time and money here.

- By using a computer you can view each image on the computer screen and print out those you choose, using high-quality glossy paper and a good colour printer. The pictures can be cropped, enhanced and sized as you wish. It is easy to insert your photos into documents or web pages, or to send them as emails.

- Using a digital camera is a costly business. As well as the expense of the camera itself (see below), to make best use of it you need a modern computer plus the appropriate software. You also need a colour inkjet printer, and for very best results should print on to expensive glossy paper. Digital cameras also use up batteries far faster than conventional cameras.

What do digital cameras cost?

The price of a digital camera is determined by its resolution, which is measured in millions of pixels (Mega-Pixels). The higher the resolution, the more expensive the camera, and the bigger print you can produce without the picture looking blocky and pixellated. If you want to play about with your shots on a computer and print them out, you should buy a high-resolution camera, which will cost around £300 or more. However, if you are buying only to put pictures on your website or email them to friends, you can buy a cheaper model costing around £150, because the resolution of your PC monitor will be the limiting factor, and you won't achieve any better results with a more costly camera.

Putting pictures on to your wedding website

There are two points to remember when putting photos or video clips on to your website:

- Do not put too many on one page, as this will slow down the speed at which the page loads. Put one or two on to a page, and use web links to step through the pages.

- Do not post the full resolution images that you get from the camera, as these will slow the site down dramatically. Instead, use your photo editing software to reduce the size of the image file (aim for a file size of 50Kb per image and no more than 100Kb per page).

To see how other couples have used pictures on the web, try searching 'wedding album' on a search engine such as Google for some examples, both good and bad, to inspire you.

Digital camcorders
Using a digital rather than an analogue camcorder does away with problems of poor resolution and grainy pictures, but you will need to pay a minimum of £500 for a digital camcorder, and many models cost much more. The recording can be played back on your television, but not on a VHS video recorder. Both digital and analogue recordings can be edited using a computer, but this can be quite complicated to set up and time-consuming to do.

Webcams
You could set up a 'live' webcam for the wedding or reception which would transmit images on to your website as they happen. A fair amount of computer and Internet expertise is required to do this, and you will also need access to a telephone line, or better still a broadband cable connection, not something that many churches or register offices can provide.

The webcam is connected to the computer, which itself is permanently logged on to the Internet. You need to set up webcam video capture software and web page posting to your web space. Special software is available but this is still a daunting task unless you are experienced.

The results are likely to be disappointing. Conventional, inexpensive webcams are generally fixed focus devices which would give a low-resolution broad view image of the venue, meaning that much detail would be lost, and viewers would not be able to recognise guests.

An alternative, although equally complex, solution, is to use a conventional camcorder with zoom lens etc. which is connected to a video 'capture card' fitted to your computer – which then transfers images to the Internet. The quality would be a little better than with a webcam, although the images are likely to be very jerky.

Chapter 8

Principal players

Your choice of best man and attendants can make a large difference to the smooth running of your wedding day. Think carefully before you decide who to ask and offer the roles to people who will enjoy performing them and whom you can trust to do a good job.

The best man

The groom usually chooses a relative or close friend for this job. Traditionally, the best man is single, but nowadays it is quite in order to choose someone who is married. The best man needs to be confident, dependable, a good organiser and someone who can be relied upon to stay sober throughout the proceedings. As well as giving practical help before, during and after the wedding, the best man is there to give moral support to the bridegroom both before the event and on the day. His responsibilities are listed below.

Before the wedding day he:

- helps the groom to choose the ushers
- organises the stag party and makes sure that the groom gets home safely after it
- arranges the hire of clothes for the groom, the ushers and himself
- attends the wedding rehearsal
- confirms all arrangements by liaising with the bride's family.

On the wedding day he:

- arranges for the honeymoon luggage to be taken to the reception venue

- briefs the ushers before going to the church
- organises the ushers at the church
- ensures buttonholes and order of service sheets are at the church
- organises parking arrangements at the church
- pays any church expenses on behalf of the groom
- drives the groom to the church, ensuring that they arrive about 40 minutes before the start of the ceremony
- takes care of the wedding ring(s) until they are needed during the ceremony
- signs the register as a witness (optional)
- accompanies the chief bridesmaid out of church
- assists the photographer in marshalling guests for photographs
- ensures that all guests have transport to the reception before leaving the church himself
- arranges his own transport to the reception
- possibly takes part in the receiving line
- generally looks after guests at the reception
- keeps an eye on the clock so that proceedings don't overrun
- keeps an eye on any wedding presents brought to the reception and ensures that they are taken away safely afterwards
- introduces the speeches and toasts, reads messages from those who could not attend, announces the cutting of the cake
- delivers his own speech
- ensures the couple have transport from the reception and, if necessary, organises a non-drinker to drive them to their destination
- ensures that honeymoon luggage is in the going-away vehicle.

After the wedding he:

- takes charge of the groom's clothes and returns any hired items promptly.

Q *I can't decide whether to ask my brother or my best friend to be best man. Can I have them both?*

A Yes, as long as you can decide between you who is going to do what. Perhaps one could perform the best man's role during the ceremony, and the other could take over at the reception.

> **Q** *I have always been very close to my sister and would like her support at my wedding. Can I have a best woman?*
>
> **A** There is no reason why a best man has to be male, although she might prefer not to come on the stag night, depending on what sort of event it is going to be.

The ushers

The number of ushers you will need depends on how many guests you invite to the ceremony. A rough guide is three ushers per 100 guests. They help seat people in the church and hand out order of service sheets. Again, choose people whom you know to be reliable and able to deal with any problems that crop up on the day. The ushers have the following duties:

- arriving at the church early
- ensuring that order of service sheets are at the front of the church for the use of the wedding party and minister
- giving buttonholes to the principal male guests
- standing at the door and distributing order of service sheets or hymn and prayer books
- directing guests to their places in church. The bride's mother and other principal guests should be personally escorted to their seats
- helping any guests with small children or those who are elderly or disabled.

The chief bridesmaid and bridal attendants

Chosen by the bride, the bridesmaids are traditionally unmarried female members of her family or close friends. However, bridesmaids and pages may also be members of the groom's family. A married attendant is known as a matron of honour.

The very young attendants are not expected to do anything on the day except look decorative and behave themselves. Do remember, however, that although tiny bridesmaids and pages can look enchanting, they cannot be relied upon to keep still and quiet during the ceremony, so choose them with care and limit the number of those under five years old. The chief bridesmaid processes up the aisle behind the bride, followed by the other attendants. If you are planning to have a flower girl, whose job it is to strew the bride's path with petals as she leaves church, do check that the minister has no objections. The chief bridesmaid is usually expected to:

- help select the bridesmaids' outfits
- organise and attend the hen party
- possibly help the bride choose her wedding dress
- help the bride to dress on the day of the wedding
- be in charge of the younger attendants, making sure they have their posies etc. and know what to do in church
- ensure the younger attendants are well-behaved in church
- arrive at the church before the bride and help arrange her dress and veil before the procession goes in
- help the bride to lift back her veil at the top of the aisle
- hold the bride's bouquet during the ceremony
- perhaps witness the signing of the register
- leave the church with the best man
- at the reception help the best man make guests welcome
- keep a check on the younger attendants at the reception
- help the bride change out of her wedding dress before leaving. She may also take charge of the bride's wedding clothes if the bride's mother is not doing this.

If you have other adult bridesmaids, they could help the chief bridesmaid with some of these jobs.

The parents of the bride and groom

The bride's father has three important duties to perform on the wedding day:

- to escort his daughter down the aisle
- to give her away during the ceremony
- to make a speech at the reception.

The bride's mother has no formal duties, and most of her work goes on behind the scenes, ensuring that everything runs smoothly.

She may play a major role in the planning and organisation of the day. If the bride is getting married from her parents' home then her mother may help her to dress on the wedding day and make sure the flowers have arrived on time and that the best man has taken the buttonholes and order of service sheets to the church.

At the reception, the bride's parents act as hosts, greeting guests and seeing that their needs are met. The groom's parents tradition-ally have much less involvement with the proceedings, although they may well contribute both financially and with any practical help that they are able to give. The two families should liaise on the guest list, and at the reception both sets of parents take part in the receiving line (if there is one), greeting guests as they arrive and making introductions where necessary.

What happens when the bride's or groom's parents are divorced?

Where neither partner of the divorced couple has remarried, then ideally they should set their differences aside and sit together in church and at the reception and stand side by side in the receiving line. If animosity makes this difficult or impossible, then they should arrange unobtrusively to have the least possible contact during the day without making the rift too uncomfortably obvious to others.

Where divorced parents have remarried, the mother sits in the first pew with her husband, and the father and his wife sit behind in the second pew. In the receiving line divorced parents should stand together, while new partners should simply mingle with the other guests.

Q *My father wants to give me away, and so does my step-father. How can we resolve this?*

A In theory, you should choose which one you feel closest to, and the other should respect your decision, which should be relayed with great tact and sensitivity. If that seems too difficult, an unconventional solution would be to ask your mother to accompany you down the aisle.

Witnesses

You will need two witnesses to sign the register at a religious or a civil wedding. The witnesses do not have to be 18, but must be old enough to understand what being a witness means. Think about who you would like to act as witnesses before the ceremony, and ask them if they would be willing. Some couples each nominate one of their parents, but you could ask a close friend, or a child from a previous marriage. Make sure that the witnesses are seated so that they can easily come up to sign the register at the appropriate moment. At a civil wedding, the registrar may ask for the witnesses to sit at the front, near the couple, for the whole of the proceedings.

Attendants at a civil ceremony

It is not usual to have bridesmaids and pages at a register office wedding, although it is not unheard of. However, you can have a best man, who can produce the rings at the appropriate moment, and the bride can ask a close relative or friend to give her special support on the day. If you marry at alternative licensed premises then you will be freer to make the occasion more like a traditional wedding and have as many attendants as you like.

Gifts from the bride and groom to the best man and attendants

It is customary to give gifts to the best man and attendants as a way of expressing your appreciation and gratitude for their contribution to your wedding day. Jewellery is a popular choice, and you could give the best man and ushers cufflinks, a tie pin or a watch, and the chief bridesmaid a necklace, ring or earrings. It is a good idea to give the same item to each of any younger bridesmaids to prevent comparisons, perhaps choosing something they can wear on the day. Watches are often popular with children and are a good choice for page boys. Ornamental keepsakes, such as a photograph frame or engraved mug, might also be suitable. Alternatively, you could break with tradition and give cameras, computers, portable CD-players or any other gift you think would be welcomed.

Many couples give the two sets of parents a gift to thank them for everything they have done to help. If you want to stick with tradition, a decorative item for the home, perhaps engraved with details of the wedding, would be appropriate, but again the rules are there to be broken, so choose what you know would be most appreciated by the people concerned.

Chapter 9

Wedding guests

The task of deciding who to invite to your wedding will be a difficult one. If your parents are making a financial contribution to the day, they will almost certainly want to have a say in who should be on the list and may insist that you invite certain relatives and family friends. You, on the other hand, may want to ask all your friends and include only close family members. This task will require diplomacy, and you will have to work out a compromise that suits everyone.

Before you start writing your list you need to work out how many people you are able to invite. Your budget and the type of reception you would like are factors that will influence this, as will the size of the wedding venue. For example, most register offices cannot accommodate more than 30 guests, in which case you could choose to invite only the closest relatives and friends to the ceremony and extend the numbers for the reception. If you have a tight budget, you could have a small family gathering for the ceremony and reception and have an informal party for friends, either at home or elsewhere, at a future date.

Having decided how many people to ask, you should make a preliminary list, starting with the people you think should definitely be invited – your closest family and friends. Then write down the names of those who you will probably ask – more distant family members and friends. Finally, list those who you would like to ask if numbers allow, such as colleagues and acquaintances. The bride and groom should have equal numbers of guests, although this might not be possible if one partner's family is much larger than the other's, for example. See Chapter 3 for advice regarding second marriages.

Inviting children

A question that inevitably arises when couples are compiling their guest list is whether or not to invite children. While some people are happy to involve them in the whole day, others are worried that they might disrupt the proceedings. The main reasons why people do not invite children are:

- they take up space on the guest list and thus limit the numbers of adults the couple can invite
- small children may get bored and may make noise during the ceremony
- their parents may find it hard work keeping them entertained during a long sit-down meal.

However, there are various solutions to these problems. You could:

- choose not to invite any children
- invite them only to the reception, in which case you should make this plain on the invitations
- provide entertainment and care for the children at the reception venue (see pages 198), and perhaps during the ceremony as well
- invite only children of very close friends and relatives, or those with whom you have a particularly close link – godchildren, for instance – and exclude others. You will need to make some tactful explanations to friends whose children are not included, but people are usually understanding of the problems.

We decided not to invite children

When Julia married Tom they were both in their forties, and almost all of their friends had children, ranging in age from 3 to 15. Julia explained why they decided not to ask any children.

'I am very close to many of the children, but we wanted to sit down in a lovely restaurant with all our best friends and have a really good meal. The food was expensive and not the sort children usually like to eat, but more importantly we knew kids would just get bored. Space was limited as well, so for each child we asked we would have had to leave out one of our friends.

'I was concerned that people would be upset or offended, or might even not come at all, so before sending any invitations I rang every friend with children and explained what we were doing and said I hoped they would understand and that it wouldn't be a problem. Most friends said they would actually prefer to come without children because then they would be able to relax and enjoy themselves more easily, and because I gave plenty of notice most people were able to make arrangements for the children to be looked after. One or two people tried to persuade us to make an exception but we had already decided not to do that. Unfortunately, my cousin and her husband decided not to come because they couldn't bring their children.

'I would advise anyone to invite children only if that's what they really want to do. If not, be sensitive to your friends' feelings, speak to them personally and explain, but be very firm and stick by your decision.'

The wedding invitations

The style of invitation you send out will set the tone for your wedding, so choose the most suitable type. A huge range of styles is available, and you can either buy them already printed (with space for you to fill in your details) from department stores and stationers, or order your own from specialist printers or stationery design companies. Look in the *Yellow Pages* or at the small ads in wedding magazines then ring or visit one or two and ask to see samples of their work and a price list. Bear in mind that an ordinary printer can usually turn round invitations far faster than a specialist wedding stationer who operates through a department store or by mail order.

Another option is to create them yourselves, either using specialist wedding software (see page 69) or a desk-top publishing system.

For a formal wedding, the invitations should be printed or engraved on good-quality white or cream card. The format is an upright, folded card measuring 14×18cm (5½×7in). Traditionally, invitations are engraved, which gives the lettering an embossed appearance, but this is expensive because a printing plate has to be made. Thermographic printing is cheaper and produces a similar result but does not look quite as smart. Flat printing is the least expensive option and produces lettering like that of a good computer printer. The print on invitations is usually black, but you could choose silver.

Quantity

You will need one invitation for each family or individual on your guest list. Etiquette demands that you also send one to the groom's parents, very close friends or relatives whom you already know will not be able to attend, the best man, attendants, and the minister and spouse (although they are unlikely to come to the reception unless they are also friends of the family). Add on another 20 or so to allow for any mistakes you may make while writing them and for any extra guests you may invite after the first replies have come in.

When to order

You will need to order your invitations at least four months in advance. This is because they take about two to four weeks to be printed and you may have to rectify any mistakes the printer might make. Traditionally, invitations are sent out six to nine weeks before the wedding, but many couples send them out earlier. Giving a deadline for a reply is useful for deciding whether or not to send out any further invitations after the first batch of replies has been received.

Wording

Work out what you want the invitations to say, then give the printer a typed sheet with the wording exactly as you want it to appear. Guests are expected to reply formally, but it can be helpful to enclose a pre-printed reply card for them to return. When you write the invitations, think carefully about how to address each guest. With formal invitations, use each person's title rather than any familiar name by which you know them, e.g. 'Mr Jack Smith' rather than 'Uncle Jack'. For informal invitations, you can address people in whatever way you choose.

Formal weddings

The traditional wording for a very formal wedding is as follows:

Mr and Mrs Mark Baxter
request the pleasure of your company/
request the honour of your presence
at the marriage of their daughter
Alice
to Mr Edward Holland
at St Mary's Church, Lymington
on (day, date, month, year)
at (time)
and afterwards at
(reception location)

RSVP
(parents'/hosts' address)

Slightly less formal, but more commonly used, is this wording:

Mr and Mrs Mark Baxter
request the pleasure of the company of
(Name of guest(s) filled in by hand)
....
at the marriage of their daughter
Alice

If the bride's parents are divorced, if either is remarried or if one of them is deceased the same basic rule applies – the hosts send the invitation, and the announcement should make it clear how the hosts and bride are related to each other. In some situations, for instance where the bride's mother has remarried and changed her name, it is helpful to include the bride's surname as well. Some alternative wordings that follow the traditional style are given below:

The bride's mother as host, when the bride's father is deceased:

Mrs David Lloyd
requests the pleasure of your company
at the marriage of her daughter

The bride's father as host, when the bride's mother is deceased:

Mr David Lloyd
requests the pleasure of your company
at the marriage of his daughter

If the bride's mother is divorced she uses her forename, Mrs Katherine Lloyd; if remarried she uses her new husband's name, Mrs James Wallace.

The bride's divorced parents as hosts, where neither has remarried:

Mr David Lloyd and Mrs Katherine Lloyd
request the pleasure of your company
at the marriage of their daughter

The bride's divorced parents as hosts, where the mother has remarried:

Mr David Lloyd and Mrs James Wallace
request the pleasure of your company
at the marriage of their daughter

The bride's mother and stepfather as hosts:

Mr and Mrs James Wallace
request the pleasure of your company
at the marriage of her daughter

The bride's father and stepmother as hosts:

Mr and Mrs David Lloyd
request the pleasure of your company
at the marriage of his daughter

The bride as host:

Miss Sally Lloyd
requests the pleasure of your company
at her marriage to

The bride and groom as hosts:

Mr Adam Jackson and Miss Sally Lloyd
request the pleasure of your company
at their marriage

Continental Europeans and members of the practising Jewish community send cards with the names of both sets of parents:

Mr and Mrs John Collins
request the pleasure of
your company at the marriage
of their daughter
Anna
to Matthew, son of Dr and Mrs Owen

For a blessing service following a civil wedding, invitations should read as follows:

Mr and Mrs John Collins
request the pleasure of your company
at the Blessing of the Marriage
of their daughter
Anna

For an invitation to the reception only, the wording is:

Mr and Mrs John Collins
request the pleasure of your company
at the Reception to celebrate the marriage
of their daughter Anna

You could include a note explaining that due to the size of the ceremony venue only a limited number of guests can be accommodated.

Informal weddings

Invitations still come from the hosts, whether the bride's family or the couple themselves, but you have a wider choice of what to say and how to say it. You can be freer with design as well and could include a sketch of the wedding venue, a photograph of yourselves, a poem or quotation or any other means you choose to personalise your invitations. Again, look at the small ads in wedding magazines for inspiration.

Typical wording, where the bride's parents are hosts, would read like this:

Mr and Mrs John Collins
invite you/have much pleasure in inviting you
to the marriage of their daughter
Anna
to Matthew Owen

If the bride and groom are hosts:

Anna Collins and Matthew Owen
(or Anna and Matthew)
invite you to their wedding

Invitation checklist

Before having your invitations printed, check whether the cost includes the envelopes. When you receive the proof, check that:

● the invitation is worded correctly
● the lines break in the right places
● the day of the week and the date match
● all the names, including those of people and venues, are spelled correctly
● the address is complete and correct
● the punctuation is correct
● the style of lettering and the type of paper are the same as those you chose.

Overnight guests

Some guests may have travelled a long way and need to stay overnight. If you are holding your reception at a hotel you may be able to arrange a deal and book several rooms at a reduced cost for these guests. Otherwise, seek out reasonable accommodation within easy reach of the venues and either offer to book for your guests or send them details so that they can make their own arrangements. This information could be included on your own website, if you have one (see page 70). *The Which? Hotel Guide*, *The Which? Guide to Country Pubs* and *The Good Bed and Breakfast Guide* all provide information about accommodation in your area.

Sending the invitations

Include clear directions and/or a map showing how to get to the wedding venue and from there to the reception. If necessary, these should be tailor-made for guests travelling from different directions. Do not enclose a wedding gift list but wait for people to ask for one to be sent. Send one invitation per family (unless the children are living away from home, say at university, in which case they should have one each) and write the names of those invited on the top left-hand corner of the invitation or fill in the space provided. Parents should assume that the invitation is for them alone if the children's names are not included.

Q *Can I use labels printed by my computer to send the invitations?*
A Not if the wedding is formal or you are concerned about using standard etiquette, which demands that envelopes be hand-written, with the correct full name and rank or title of the guest.

> **Tip**
>
> You might like to have a 'wedding book' at the reception, which all your guests are asked to sign and which will make a good souvenir of the day. Let people know in advance that the book will be provided so that they can think of an appropriate message. At the end of his speech the best man could remind the guests to sign the book and tell them exactly where they can find it.
>
> Books specifically designed for this purpose are sold in department stores but you could use any book with blank pages. One option would be to buy a leather-bound book with blank pages and have your names and the date of your wedding embossed on the front.

Postponing the wedding

Occasionally circumstances demand that the wedding be delayed. You do not need to return wedding gifts if the wedding is postponed to a future date. Cards should be sent to guests telling them of the postponement and giving details of the new date if it is known. For details of what to do if the engagement is broken and the wedding cancelled, see pages 18–19.

Suitable wording for a printed notification of postponement would read as follows:

Owing to the recent illness/death
of Mrs Collins' father
the wedding of her daughter
Anna
to Matthew Owen
at (venue, time)
on (date)
has been postponed
until (time)
on (date)

Guest checklist

Name	Address	Tel.	No. in party	Invitation sent	Accepted	Refused

Chapter 10

Wedding gifts

As soon as you have sent out your invitations people will start to ask you what you would like as a wedding gift. Although your guests are not obliged to give you anything (which is why it is impolite to enclose the list with the invitation), almost all of them will want to buy you something they know you will be pleased to receive. One way of ensuring you are given the things you need and avoid duplication is to organise a list, either your own or at a store. However, you are not forced to have a list and can leave the choice up to your guests. For a small wedding or where the partners have been living together for some time, this may be a straightforward solution.

Making your own list

One way to draw up a list is to browse round a number of different shops, picking out items you would like to receive. Type up an informative list, including details of size, colour, manufacturer, model number and price. Include delivery instructions against any large items. Either the bride's mother, the couple or even the groom's mother could take charge of the list. When guests ask to see it you can send the master copy with a stamped addressed envelope and ask them to cross off the item they choose and return the list or send it on. This method is cumbersome but does avoid duplication. A quicker method is to have several copies of the list and send one to any guest who asks. You may end up with some duplication but the whole process is speeded up and there is no danger of the list getting stuck with one person who then holds everyone else up. Finally, you could give the phone number of the person in charge of the list to any guests who ask so that they can ring up and find out what is on the list. The guests can then ask the holder to cross off a particular gift before buying it.

Putting your list with a store

Many couples prefer to place their list with one or perhaps two department stores. If most of your guests are local you could choose one in the nearest town. However, if they live in different parts of the UK you could choose a chain that has branches nationwide.

How you go about setting up your list depends on which store you place it at. Usually, you visit the store and either look through the catalogue or walk round the shop, noting which items you would like (writing down the description, size, colour, price and code). Some stores will produce as many copies of the list as you need to send to guests, while others prefer to keep the master list so that the guests have to ring up or visit to find out what is available. Whichever method the store uses, the guests then tell the store which gift they have bought or want to buy, and the store then crosses it off the list. The stores, which are computer-linked if part of a chain, keep the list up to date and note who has bought what. They then inform you of what has been bought so that you can start writing thank-you letters.

You could put a list at more than one store, choosing one for household, practical gifts and another for more decorative or specialised items. Some stores offer incentives, such as gift vouchers or discounts, if you place your list with them, so it can often be worth shopping around before choosing one.

Gift list considerations

- List more items than there are guests, otherwise the last people to see the list will not have a choice.
- Choose items across the price range so that every guest can buy something within his or her means.
- Don't worry if some of the items you have chosen are very expensive as some people like to join up with friends and buy something more expensive than they could afford as an individual.

Delivery

Before you set up your list, ask how the gifts will be delivered to you. In some stores guests simply buy their gift and take it home ready to send to you or bring on the day. Other stores will deliver the gifts to you as they are purchased or will keep them all and deliver them after the wedding, notifying you of who has bought what in the meantime.

Q *Can I exchange a gift that I don't like?*

A If the same item is accidentally purchased twice or if you change your mind after receiving the gift, most stores will exchange it for something of the same value provided the item has not been used.

Compiling a wedding list

Couples who are setting up home for the first time will not need any help in drawing up a long list of things they need. However, for those who do need some help, wedding magazines provide lists of suggestions and you will find lots of useful gift sites and catalogues on the Internet. Leave yourselves plenty of time as choosing the right items for every part of the house requires a great deal of thought, and the list needs to be ready about seven to ten weeks before the wedding.

The question of gifts is more difficult for the high percentage of couples who have lived together before marriage or who have been married before, as they will have most household items already. So, if you are past the stage of needing saucepans and cutlery, here are a few suggestions:

- decorative items: pictures, plants, hand-embroidered cushions, antiques
- vintage wines
- luxury food items
- CDs or videos
- sports equipment

- plants for your garden
- tickets to a show or for travel
- gift vouchers for a specified store
- cash is increasingly acceptable as a gift suggestion
- unit trusts, shares, Premium Bonds
- donations to a specified charity.

Thank-you letters

Write a letter of thanks for each gift as it arrives; if you let them accumulate the task will seem much more daunting. Keep an up-to-date list (see overleaf) and make a note when the thank-you letter has been sent. You should send a hand-written letter for every gift you receive, even if you have already thanked the giver in person. Some gifts will be received on, or after, the day, and you should send thank-you letters for these as soon as you return from honeymoon.

The letter need not be long but should be specific about the gift so that if, for instance, the store has delivered the wrong number of bowls the person concerned can put things right. If you receive money or vouchers, tell the giver how you plan to use them.

For gifts given jointly by two or three people, write to each one separately. A present given by a large group of people such as work colleagues needs only one letter, addressed to the group as a whole.

Displaying the gifts

The custom of displaying the wedding gifts is becoming less common. However, if you do decide on a display, make sure the reception venue has somewhere secure, preferably out of sight of public areas, where the gifts can be shown. Group similar items such as glasses, linen etc. together, although if two items are nearly identical it is more tactful to place them apart. Cheques should be acknowledged by placing cards on the display table saying 'Cheque from Mr and Mrs John Smith'. You should not state the amount.

You will probably receive a number of gifts on the wedding day. Make sure that you have a safe place to put these and detail one of the bridesmaids to be responsible for keeping labels and cards with the gifts to which they belong. See Chapter 21 for details of how to make sure your wedding gifts are protected wherever they are.

Gift checklist

Name of guest	Gift list sent	Gift received	Thank-you letter sent

Chapter 11

Wedding outfits

What you, the best man, ushers and attendants wear will depend on the wedding venue and how formal/informal your ceremony is going to be.

The bride

Choosing an outfit in which you will look and feel right on the day is one of the most important, enjoyable decisions you will make in the run-up to the ceremony. If you are lucky enough to know what you are looking for, the only issue is finding it or having it made for you. Otherwise, start your search by taking a careful look at every wedding picture you see – in magazines, local newspapers, photographers' windows and advertisements.

Traditional wedding dresses

Buying

You can buy your wedding dress off-the-peg at any number of specialist bridal shops or department stores. Start your hunt early. Most bridal stores and departments stock samples only, and your dress will be ordered specially and could take between 12 and 16 weeks to arrive. You should also allow some time on top of this for any alterations that then have to be made.

When you shop, it is a good idea to make an appointment with a dress shop. Do this as far in advance as you can, and try to avoid Saturdays, as this is when popular shops can get booked up for several months ahead. Appointments usually last about an hour, and are with a fitter who can help you to get dresses on and off, and can find the accessories to go with them. You should have time to try on up to 15 dresses.

For a cheaper alternative, have a look at some evening gowns. Many of these could readily be worn as a wedding dress (or might suit an adult bridesmaid), and they often cost far less than a 'proper' wedding dress. Try on lots of different styles, including those that do not particularly appeal when on the hanger (often they look much better when you try them on). Wear make-up and arrange your hair in a similar style to the one you would like to have on the day so you can get a good idea of how the dress will really look. Ask someone whose opinions you trust to go with you.

Tip

If you can shop well in advance of your wedding day you might be able to pick up an end-of-season bargain, for example you could buy an end-of-season summer dress in the autumn to wear the following summer. Most shops bring in new ranges once or twice a year and sell off the remains of previous ranges. These sales are often advertised in local newspapers.

Buying secondhand

Look in the *Yellow Pages* or in the small ads in wedding magazines for shops that specialise in secondhand gowns. Many dresses are sold privately through advertisements in local newspapers or specialist advertisements-only magazines such as *Loot*. Expect to pay about half of what the dress originally cost. Some dresses are sold unworn, and the rest may have been worn only once.

Having a dress made

Having a dress made will not necessarily be cheaper than buying a ready-made one – unless you can persuade a dressmaking friend or relative to make it for you – but you are more likely to get exactly what you want, and the dress will be made to fit you rather than being a 'standard' dress size (an important consideration if you fall between sizes or you are particularly short or tall, for example). Excluding the cost of the fabric, you can expect to pay from £250 for having a simple style made up, to as much as £3,000 for a very elaborate confection with a lot of fine detail which has to be sewn by hand.

Finding a dressmaker

If you know someone who wore a made-to-measure dress that you admired, finding out who their dressmaker was is probably the best starting point – not least because if that dressmaker is already fully booked, she (or he) should know of other dressmakers for you to contact. If you do not have any personal recommendations, try the *Yellow Pages* (under 'Dressmakers' and possibly 'Wedding services'). Alternatively, look in the small ads section at the back of wedding magazines and also the bridal magazines published by pattern companies such as Vogue, Butterick, Simplicity and so on. For a small fee, the Butterick Company (of which Vogue Patterns is a subsidiary) can supply a list of dressmakers in your area. Other pattern companies may offer a similar service.

If you have Internet access, you can also find a designer or dressmaker in your area by using the Designer Directory.* If you can't find a local dressmaker, you could also consider using the mail order service offered by Bridal Wear by Design* and JMD Style,* both of which will make up the pattern of your choice or design a dress specially for you. You can also get details of having a dress made to measure by going to Elegance Bridal Wear.*

Getting the best from your dressmaker

When you find a dressmaker who seems suitable, ask to see examples of her (or his) work. If you are happy with what you see and the dressmaker is willing to take you on, you should arrange a meeting to talk about what you want. Take along pictures of the kind of dresses and accessories that you particularly like. These will give the dressmaker an idea of your likes and dislikes, which will, in turn, help her (or him) to come up with suitable designs for you. Before the first meeting it is also well worth your while visiting the off-the-peg wedding dress shops to try on dresses, veils and headdresses so that you get a good feel for what suits you (and what does not).

The next step will be for your dressmaker to show you a selection of sketches based on the ideas you discussed at the first consultation. If you like them and you feel comfortable about working with the dressmaker in what are going to be quite intimate situations, the next thing you need to know is how much it is going to cost. If, on the other hand, the sketches bear no relation to your dream dress and you feel that the dressmaker has not listened to any of your ideas, this may be the time to look for someone else: you will not feel your best on your wedding day if you have been bullied into wearing something that doesn't really suit you.

Tip

Long trains can be cumbersome at the reception, so if you are having a train, make sure it is detachable so it can be removed after the ceremony. Some dresses have a loop fixed on to the train so that the bride can hook it over her wrist and prevent it from trailing on the ground.

What will it cost?

The two main influences on the final cost of your dress are the fabric and your dressmaker's time. Clearly, the more fabric involved and the more expensive it is, the costlier the final dress will be. How much your dressmaker's time will cost depends on how elaborate the design is, whether it involves a lot of intricate hand sewing and how many fittings are necessary. The final cost will also be influenced by the number of times you change your mind about what you want, which is why many dressmakers can be reticent about putting a price on their work until it is completed – although most will be able to give you a rough guide.

If the estimated price sounds reasonable, you will need to agree (preferably in writing):

- exactly what the dressmaker is supplying – just the dress, for example, or the dress and other accessories
- the delivery date
- dates for fittings
- a schedule for payments – whether you will pay a deposit and make a final payment, for example, or whether you will need to make interim payments as well (which may be the case if some

special detail, such as hand embroidery or covered buttons, will be subcontracted)

- who will pay for the fabric – this is usually the customer, although the dressmaker will usually supply routine haberdashery such as thread, binding, zips and so on
- whether VAT is payable and, if it is, whether it is included in the quoted price.

Choosing the fabric

Be guided by your dressmaker's specialist knowledge when it comes to choosing the material for your dress: she (or he) will know which fabrics are best suited to achieving the look you want. She (or he) will also know the best sources of bridal fabrics at competitive prices – shops specialising in bridal fabric can be in the most unexpected places and are rarely to be found on the high street. If you have a particular fabric in mind, your dressmaker can also advise you on which styles will work best (make sure that you take a sample of it to your first meeting).

Making it fit

Before your first fitting, it is a good idea to buy your wedding underwear and, once you have the fabric to match them to, your shoes. Getting the right underwear is particularly important for very close-fitting styles and having the shoes is vital for getting the length right. A good dressmaker is unlikely to cut the fabric until she (or he) has fitted you for a 'toile' (a test garment usually made out of cotton). Depending on your chosen style, subsequent fittings may involve getting component parts right so don't expect to see the final product until quite late on in the process.

Having a dress altered to fit

A dressmaker can also alter an existing dress to fit you. You might need to have this done if you have bought a secondhand or off-the-peg dress that doesn't fit you exactly or if you want to wear your mother's or grandmother's dress, for example.

Having a dress altered is also worth considering if you are on a tight budget, especially if you have an eye for a bargain and you manage to pick up a nearly-suitable dress in the sales or in a second-hand or charity shop.

Making your dress yourself

If you have little or no experience of dressmaking but are drawn to the idea of making the dress yourself because you are on a tight budget, you should consider the following practicalities before making up your mind:

- **have you got a sewing machine?** If not, don't assume that you will be able to borrow one unless you have a firm offer of a loan
- **have you worked out what the material will cost?** It may be that once you have added up the cost of the dress fabric, other material for linings, petticoats, stiffening and haberdashery, you will find that it is not quite as cheap as you thought it was going to be
- **where are you going to cut it out?** You need a large, level, scrupulously clean surface (not carpet) to cut out a long frock accurately
- **where are you going to sew it?** You need somewhere that is well-lit, clean and preferably away from anything that could get spilt on the dress – so the kitchen table is not ideal
- **how are you going to alter it to fit?** Unless you have the help of another person or a tailor's dummy, it will be very difficult to get a good fit on your own
- **do you have a full-length mirror?** Fitting will be nearly impossible if you have not
- **are you familiar with pattern instructions?** It might be an idea to look through the instruction sheets of a wedding dress pattern before you commit yourself. Even if you have to buy the pattern to do this, it will be cheaper than possibly ruining a lot of expensive material
- **do you have back-up?** Unless you have a friend or relative who is willing to help out and/or advise you when you hit a tricky patch or make a mistake, it is probably not a good idea to tackle the job
- **could you make the bridesmaids' dresses instead?** This could be a good compromise because the dresses will be less crucial and, especially if you are having young children as your bridesmaids, more manageable to make.

If you decide that your wedding dress is something you can tackle and you have someone who will help if the need arises, it would be a good idea to invest in one or more of the special bridal magazines published by pattern companies. Not only will they have suitable patterns, but you will also find that they have addresses both of shops selling bridal fabrics and companies which sell fabric (often more cheaply) by mail order.

If, having considered the practicalities, you decide that it would not be a good idea to start practising your sewing skills on your wedding dress, there are still several options open to you – such as borrowing, hiring, having a dress altered or buying secondhand.

Tip

After the wedding you can have your dress expertly cleaned and packed in acid-free tissue. Materials are also available to do the packing yourself. Some companies sell special boxes and tissue – complete with instructions on how to pack the dress away properly. Look in bridal magazines for addresses.

Hiring

Hiring is a less popular option than it used to be but it is still possible from some department stores or specialist shops. You will need to give about 12 weeks' notice and should be able to collect the dress a couple of days before the wedding for return two days after. Check:

- that the dress will be available on your wedding day (get this in writing)
- that minor alterations are possible
- that the fee includes insurance against damage and cost of cleaning
- how many days the hire cost covers
- what alternatives are on offer if the dress is unavailable for any reason.

Veils, headdresses and hats

Veils vary in price depending on the length, amount of decoration and type of fabric, which might be silk or nylon tulle, lace or organza. The general rule is that if your dress has a train you wear a full-length veil, which falls to the ground and is about a foot longer than your train. Otherwise, you can have a short, face-framing veil, one that skims your shoulders or reaches to your fingertips, and it can be worn piled high on a headdress or falling simply from a band or tiara. Try on a range of styles with your chosen dress and remember that how you wear your hair on the day can alter the look significantly.

A headdress can be worn with or without a veil. Once again, bridal magazines and shops will supply plenty of ideas, from simple circlets and Alice bands to tiaras. Floral headdresses are also popular (see page 112). You might prefer to wear a hat rather than a veil, in which case you could choose not to carry a bouquet.

Shoes

In winter white or pale-coloured shoes may be hard to come by outside specialist bridal shops, so buy them in spring or summer if you can. Shoes can be dyed or covered to get an exact match for your dress. Make sure the shoes are comfortable as well as stylish, since you will be on your feet for the greater part of the day. Very high heels can be hard to cope with under a full length dress, especially if you are not used to them. Wear the shoes round the house so that they ease to the shape of your foot, and rub the soles with sandpaper or a metal-bristled suede brush to make sure there is no danger of slipping.

Underwear

Choose a well-fitting bra in a flesh tone and try it on with your dress to ensure that neither the bra nor straps can be seen. Wear the bra for a few hours before the day to make sure it is really comfortable and does not ride up or slip down. Tights or stockings will fit better if they have been washed once. Buy two pairs just in case one is laddered as you put it on.

Other accessories

Make sure your car hire includes a white umbrella so that you can get into church without getting wet if it rains. Shawls, wraps, coats and cloaks can all be an integral part of your wedding outfit. Gloves may fit with your style of wedding dress but remember that your left hand will need to be uncovered during the ceremony. You do not have to carry flowers and could instead hold a prayer book or Bible, a fan or a small bag.

Tip

Ask the chief bridesmaid or your mother to carry an emergency repair kit containing tiny safety pins, needle and thread, spare tights, headache pills, tissues, comb and make-up.

Outfits for a civil wedding

A civil wedding allows you more freedom of choice, especially if you are marrying at alternative premises, such as a hotel or stately home. If you do decide to wear traditional bridal dress for a register office wedding, choose a fairly simple style without a train.

Alternatively, you can choose a smart dress or suit. You can opt for pastel colours, cream or ivory but there is no reason why you shouldn't wear a stronger colour if that's what suits you best. You could also wear a hat. If you have decided to have a themed wedding to suit the surroundings you could even wear medieval, Tudor or Victorian dress.

What to wear for a beach wedding

- Tight-fitting garments will feel uncomfortably hot. Choose light-weight cotton or crêpe de chine fabrics in a loose style.
- Open sandals or bare feet are most comfortable. Enclosed shoes will make your feet hot and likely to swell, and heels will sink into the sand.
- Pack your outfits carefully with plenty of tissue paper and hang them in a steamy bathroom for 15 minutes on arrival to let the creases drop out.

Going-away outfits

This is the outfit into which you will change before leaving the reception, although if you wear a very lavish wedding dress and have a long reception with dancing you may want to change earlier in the evening so that you can dance in comfort. Otherwise, the choice is yours and you can wear a dress, a suit or something more casual. What you wear can depend on where you are going after the reception. If you are flying off on honeymoon that day then comfortable clothes in uncrushable fabrics that will suit the climate of your destination are the obvious choice. If, however, you are spending a night at a hotel you can choose a dressy outfit that will look good in photographs as you leave but which can be worn again in future.

The groom

For a very formal church wedding the groom usually wears morning dress or a suit. The couple's fathers, the best man and the ushers should wear the same style of dress as the groom.

Traditional morning dress consists of a black or grey three-piece suit with tail coat, or black tail coat with grey pinstripe trousers and a grey waistcoat. The morning dress is worn with a wing-collared shirt and cravat, or an ordinary collar and tie. Make sure all the men in the wedding party know exactly what combination you have chosen so they can all wear the same.

You can choose a patterned or coloured cravat, waistcoat or cummerbund, which might pick up a colour from the bride's bouquet or the bridesmaids' dresses. Morning dress is extremely expensive to buy, and most men choose to hire it. Go to a reputable company well in advance for a fitting. Expect to pick it up a couple of days in advance and arrange for it to be returned within two days after the wedding.

Check whether cleaning is included in the price. All the accessories will also be available for hire. These include grey gloves, which traditionally are carried, not worn, and a silk top hat, which is worn only for some of the photographs. You can also hire tiepins or cufflinks, but most men prefer to use their own. Wear a pair of comfortable and smart black shoes.

Two- or three-piece lounge suits are the usual alternative to morning dress for less formal church or civil weddings. Colour and style are entirely your choice. If you are wearing a dark suit, you could wear a colourful tie, shirt or waistcoat. The best man should also wear a lounge suit, which should complement the groom's outfit but need not be an exact match.

If you are getting married on a beach abroad, you need not wear jacket or tie. Trousers or shorts in cotton or linen, worn with a cool shirt would be fine.

The bridegroom can leave the reception wearing the same lounge suit he wore for the wedding or if he wore morning dress he can change into a jacket and tie with smart trousers or perhaps just a shirt and casual trousers.

Bridesmaids and page boys

The first decision you need to make is whether to buy, make or hire the outfits. They could come from the same source as the bride's dress, or the adult bridesmaids may be happy to make their own dresses or buy them off-the-peg from a department store or bridal shop. Decide on your budget and who will pay. Traditionally, the bride's family pay for the attendants' clothes, but bridesmaids or, if they are children, their parents, may be happy to contribute or bear the whole cost, particularly if you choose styles which can be worn again for parties. Make it clear when you ask them to be bridesmaids who is going to pay for their outfits.

Choosing a style

The bridesmaids' dresses could be similar to your wedding dress but not identical, for example if yours has a full skirt their dresses could be straight but with the same neckline or sleeves as yours. Alternatively, they could be almost identical in style but in a different colour and without beading or other detail that yours might have.

The adult and young bridesmaids do not have to wear the same styles as each other, for example the older girls could wear straight dresses while the younger ones wear dresses that are fuller in style. Another option could be to dress the children in a paler shade of the colour the adult bridesmaids are wearing or make the older bridesmaids' dresses one solid colour and the smaller girls' dresses cream or ivory with trimmings in your chosen colour.

Page boys could wear velvet suits or lounge-style suits with waistcoat, sailor suits or Scottish outfits with kilt and sporran. Miniature morning suits for children are available to hire.

The bride's mother

At a formal wedding the bride's mother has an important and prominent role to play as hostess. Her outfit should be chosen so that it does not clash with the bride's colour scheme, and although her clothes should be attractive and eye-catching they should not draw attention away from the bride. It is advisable for her to confer with the groom's mother before shopping so that they avoid wearing outfits that are too similar or that will not look good together in photographs. Large-brimmed hats can overshadow the face in pictures and cast unflattering shadows, so the style should be chosen with care.

Chapter 12

Flowers

To find a suitable florist, look in the *Yellow Pages* or local newspapers, or consult the wide range of wedding magazines now available. Sometimes photographers or hairdressers have free leaflets listing local companies that offer wedding services, but probably the best source is personal recommendation. Most florists have a portfolio of their wedding designs and will be happy to discuss these with you. A growing number of florists use the Internet to advertise their businesses and illustrate their arrangements.

As florists are always very busy during the summer months, you should book well in advance, although you do not need to think in detail about your flowers until you have chosen your outfit and colour scheme. Arrange to meet the florist a couple of months before the wedding to go through the arrangements in detail and make some firm decisions.

The initial meeting

- Take with you any **inspirational pictures** you have collected. Even if the flowers in a bouquet you admire are difficult to get hold of at the time of year you are getting married, the florist should be able to achieve a similar effect using different flowers.
- Take **swatches of fabric from your dress** and the bridesmaids' outfits if possible, plus sketches or photographs of the styles. These will help the florist to choose a style of bouquet to suit your dress.
- Any **colour or combination of colours is acceptable**, but if you choose white flowers be careful, as it can be hard to match

the shade with that of your dress. For example, a bluish-white dress would make creamy flowers look drab and discoloured.

- Work out **how much you want to spend on your flowers** so you can give the florist an idea of the size of your order. You should also have given some thought to how many buttonholes and corsages you need and where you would like to place flowers in the wedding venue and at the reception.

Which flowers?

Although most flowers are now available all year round (thanks to hothouse production) they are always more expensive out of season. Many flowers have traditional meanings, which you might like to take into account when making up your bouquet. Several of the flowers listed overleaf, such as chrysanthemums and roses, are available across several seasons.

The bouquets

Hand-tied bouquets are currently very popular and can vary in style a great deal, depending on the shape and size and choice of flowers and foliage. They are very striking and are more readily available than the more formal wired bouquets, but can be heavy and cumbersome. Other options include a single flower or a tight ball (pomander).

Keep the style of your dress in mind when choosing your bouquet. Bodice detail may be hidden if it is behind a large bouquet, and you might prefer an arrangement that can be held in the crook of your arm. Shorter, simpler dresses call for smaller bouquets, while a tailored gown with a train can be just as beautifully offset by half a dozen lilies as by a more complex and sophisticated arrangement.

The bridesmaids' flowers should complement the bride's bouquet and are usually smaller posies using the same flowers. Very young bridesmaids may tire of holding a bouquet, so you could give them a pomander or flowers in small baskets to carry; these can both be looped over the arm.

Seasonal flowers and their meanings

Spring

apple blossom	good luck in the future
camellia	perfect loveliness
carnation	deep love
daffodil	regard
daisy	innocence
honeysuckle	devotion
iris	burning love
jasmine	grace
lily	purity
mimosa	sensitivity
tulip	love
white lilac	youthful innocence

Summer

cornflower	hope
lily of the valley	renewed happiness
rose	love, happiness
red rose	I love you
white rose	I am worthy of you
sweetpea	delicate pleasures

Autumn

red chrysanthemum	I love you
white chrysanthemum	truth
gypsophila	fertility
orchid	beauty

Winter

snowdrop	hope
ivy	fidelity

> **Preserving your bouquet**
>
> If you want to toss your bouquet into the crowd as you leave, you might want to extract one or two flowers first and ask someone to press them for you as a souvenir. You can also arrange to have the whole bouquet preserved. The bouquet is photographed and the flowers dismantled petal by petal. These are then pressed and mounted on silk. Prices depend on the size of the finished picture. The cost of pressing the flowers (and picking them up by courier) is £55, and the picture costs between £30 and £260. A company called Pressed for Time* offers a nationwide service. Alternatively, a florist may be able to make a replica of your bouquet using silk flowers.

Floral headdresses

Floral headdresses – in the form of a circlet or coronet – are an imaginative alternative to tiaras, circlets or Alice bands. Flowers can also be attached to a hair band, wired or even woven into your hair. Ask your florist's advice on which varieties to use as some wilt far more readily than others. All fresh flowers are susceptible to heat, however, and may lose their freshness as the day wears on. Try to handle them as little as possible while your hair is being arranged.

Buttonholes and corsages

Buttonholes are worn by all the men in the wedding party – groom, best man, the ushers and the couple's fathers. Traditionally, the men wear a white or cream carnation or rose. However, you do not need to feel restricted to these flowers and you can choose any colour or flower you like to match those in your bouquet or pick up a shade from your colour scheme.

Corsages are worn by the mothers of the bride and groom and consist of two or three flowers and some foliage. Consult the wearers about their preferred colours and weight, because it may not be possible to attach a heavy corsage to a light silk outfit, for example, without damaging the fabric.

Flowers for a religious ceremony

You should discuss the church flowers with the minister when you first meet. Most will be happy for you to provide your own flowers (you might be able to ask the regular church flower arranger to do them for you in return for a contribution to the church funds), while others have a policy of supplying all the floral arrangements. Alternatively, you could make use of the flowers that have been arranged for the Sunday service or choose not to have any at all.

Where to put flowers for the ceremony

In church, with the minister's permission, you can place flowers in some or all of the following sites:

- altar (some ministers prefer to leave this bare so that the cross remains the focal point)
- pulpit
- lectern
- windowsills
- font (may not be allowed, particularly if there is a christening the following day)
- columns
- church entrance
- chancel steps
- pew ends
- lych gate.

In a synagogue, flowers may be used on the *chuppah*.

Often more than one wedding is held on the same day, making it impossible to change the flowers. If this is the case, the cost of the flowers is usually divided between couples, and you should all meet with the church helpers to discuss what type of flowers would best suit you all.

Flowers for a civil ceremony

Most register offices keep an arrangement of fresh flowers permanently on display. Ask at your first visit whether you can bring in flowers of your own, as policies vary. On a busy day, when one wedding follows quite rapidly after another, there may not be time to set up new flowers. If you are marrying at an approved licensed venue, such as a hotel or stately home, then you should be able to use as many flowers as you wish.

Flowers for the reception

Some reception venues include a number of floral arrangements as part of the overall cost. Check this when you are making your booking. Most will be happy for you to provide your own flowers. Alternatively, you may be able to arrange for the transport of your own large pedestal arrangements from the church for further display at the reception venue.

Where to put flowers at the reception

- at the entrance to the room
- elsewhere in the main room – on sills or side tables
- on the buffet table
- on each dining table, with a more elaborate arrangement for the top table. The main table could also be dressed with swags or garlands of flowers
- on top of the cake and on the cake table
- on pedestals around the room or marquee
- in hanging baskets if you are having a marquee
- spiralling up the columns of a marquee
- on the banisters.

You could either continue the floral theme from your bouquet and wedding venue or choose a totally different style, using other colours and flowers. If your florist is arranging the flowers at the reception, he or she will want to know:

- when the flower arrangers can have access to the reception venue
- if there is another booking immediately before or after yours and, if there is, when the flowers must be removed. One option could be for the people using the room after you to use your flowers and contribute to the cost
- (if you are using a marquee) the colour of the lining, whether or not it has poles or a covered walkway that need decorating and, if so, how many there are

- (if you are using a marquee) whether you want to use pedestals or have hanging baskets and how many of them you need. (The marquee company will need to provide rope to attach the hanging baskets.) The benefit of having hanging baskets is that although pedestals look beautiful to the first few guests who enter the room, if it is a stand-up reception, they will not be seen by many people once the room is full. Hanging baskets will be visible to everyone throughout the proceedings.

Flowers checklist

Name of florist						
Address						
Telephone/fax						
Contact						
Date booking made						
Confirmed in writing						

	Colour	Type of flowers	No.	Delivery details	Who pays?	Cost £
Bride's bouquet						
Bridesmaids' bouquets						
Adults						
Children						
Headdresses						
Bride						

Adult bridesmaids														
Child bridesmaids														
Buttonholes														
Groom														
Best man														
Ushers														
Couple's fathers														
Others														
Corsages														
Bride's mother														
Groom's mother														
Flowers in wedding venue														
Altar														
Pulpit														
Lectern														
Windowsills														
Font														

Columns											
Entrance											
Chancel steps											
Pew ends											
Lych gate											
Chuppah											
Reception flowers											
Entrance											
Hanging baskets											
Pedestals											
Covered walkway											
Cake table											
Head table											
Buffet table											
Any other flowers											
VAT											
Total cost											

Chapter 13

Transport

Most people who have a formal white wedding in a church, synagogue or approved licensed premises hire at least one chauffeur-driven car and, more usually, two. Hired wedding cars are comfortable and roomy, allowing the bride to travel to the ceremony in style and with her dress uncrushed. The bride's mother and attendants, who travel together, leave the house first and wait for the bride in the church porch. The second car takes the bride and her father (or person giving her away) from the house to the church. It is up to the best man to arrange for the groom to arrive at the church in plenty of time (usually about 40 minutes before the ceremony).

After the ceremony, the bride and groom leave for the reception in one car, followed by the bride's parents and possibly the attendants in the second. You need to think through the transport arrangements well in advance to make sure that suitable transport is available for everyone. On the day it is the best man's job to make sure that everyone can get to the reception without difficulty.

For a register office wedding the arrangements are usually less formal, and bride and groom can arrive together if they wish. You can use hire cars, private family cars or taxis.

Wedding cars

Hired cars are the most popular choice, and a wide variety are on offer, ranging from vintage Rolls-Royces and Daimlers, through American Cadillacs and stretch limousines, to open-topped E-type Jaguars. Personal recommendation is the best way to find a reliable hire company, otherwise you should try the *Yellow Pages* or a wedding magazine.

Book your transport well in advance and expect to pay at least £250, possibly substantially more for something unusual. Cars are usually decorated with white or cream ribbons, but if you want flowers or other decorations you may have to arrange these yourselves. When choosing the cars bear in mind that a white dress can look dull in front of a white car, and it may look better if you choose one in a darker colour such as maroon, navy blue or black. Many companies offer a complete package tailored to your requirements for the day.

Remember:

- visit the company and see the cars for yourself
- ensure that the car you see is the one you will get, not a similar one or a different model. Confirm this in writing
- ask whether the car is a genuine vintage, i.e. made between 1917 and 1930, or veteran, which can either be pre-1916 or pre-1905. Cars made 'in the style of' older cars can look effective and should be cheaper to hire than an original
- inspect the general condition of the car: tyres, seating, woodwork, paintwork etc.
- ask if ribbons or flowers are included in the price
- check that a large umbrella in cream or white comes with the car
- the law requires you to wear a seatbelt in the front and back of a modern car, but vintage and veteran cars and some classic models have them in the front only or not at all. If the car was made before the seatbelt laws were enforced you are exempt from wearing them. This could be an important factor to consider if your dress is likely to be creased by a belt
- ask for written confirmation of the cars to be provided, date and times, whether a chauffeur is provided (and if so, what uniform he or she will wear), insurance cover and any extra charges
- the confirmation should include an assurance that the cars will be used only for your wedding on that date and not for any others on the same day. This is because you do not want to find that your car is late picking you up because it was delayed at a previous wedding.

Borrowing cars

If you do not want to spend so much on your transport, you could ask whether family and friends have any suitable cars that you could borrow for the day. They might also be willing to act as chauffeur for you. Give the cars a thorough clean and polish and decorate them with ribbons and flowers. Do make sure that there is room for you to get in and out comfortably in your wedding dress. Although open-topped cars sound attractive, the wind can wreak havoc with your hair and veil unless you travel exceptionally slowly.

Parking arrangements

Find out in advance what the parking regulations are at both the ceremony and reception venues, particularly if either is in a busy town. If no large car parks are available at the venue itself, check out other nearby car parks and include their details and perhaps a map with your invitations.

Other forms of transport

Horse-drawn carriages, with optional liveried coachmen and foot-men or pageboys, or closed carriages, with heated interiors for winter, are also available. Book well in advance for these, as popular summer dates can be booked up as much as two years in advance. This mode of transport, although romantic, is feasible only if the journey is fairly short and does not include any steep hills. In an open carriage you will be at the mercy of the weather, so you need to be reasonably confident of a fine day. Most companies offer a choice of colour of the horses. Expect to pay between £400 and £800, depending on the distance, number of horses and the type of carriage.

Leaving the reception

Traditionally, it is up to the best man to ensure that the newly-weds have the means of transport to leave the reception. This may be the groom's own car, left at the reception venue earlier. If fun-loving guests or ushers decide to 'decorate' the car it is up to the best man to make sure that it is not damaged and any embellishments can be easily removed. You can use one of your hire cars again, particularly if the reception has been a short one, but a private car or taxi is probably more suitable, especially as the cost per hour of a hired car is high.

Those wanting to leave in style could consider:

- a hot-air balloon (only possible when the weather is calm, and exactly where you will land cannot be guaranteed)
- motorbike with side car
- tandem bicycle
- rickshaw
- boat, from a waterside reception
- black taxi cab.

Transport hire checklist

Name of hire company	
Address	
Telephone/fax/email	
Contact	
Date booking made	
Number of cars booked	
Other modes of transport booked (horse and carriage etc.)	
Confirmed in writing	
Cost £	
Deposit £	
Balance due £	

Chapter 14

Music and readings for the ceremony

Adding carefully chosen music and readings is a way of making your ceremony more personal.

Religious ceremony

Music creates a memorable atmosphere for your wedding ceremony and is used:

- before the bride arrives (the prelude)
- as she walks down the aisle (the processional)
- while the register is being signed
- as the married couple leave the church (the recessional).

Two or three hymns and perhaps a psalm are also usually sung during the service.

Discuss the music the first time you meet the minister. Most churches are equipped with an organ, and the organist will be able to suggest suitable pieces if you need some ideas. Bear in mind the organist's abilities and the quality of the organ when making a selection. You will usually have to pay between £50 and £80 if the church organist plays for you. If a family member or friend is an accomplished organist, it should be possible to arrange for him or her to play at the ceremony instead.

You might like to have a choir to lead the singing during your service and perhaps sing a piece of your choice while you are signing the register. Some churches have their own choir, which you can hire for a small fee (probably no more than £100 and possibly less), but you could hire a professional choir or one from a local school instead.

The selection of pieces suitable for weddings is wide, and your local record library or shop should be able to provide some compilation recordings to help you choose. You do not have to restrict yourselves to religious pieces – but do check that your minister has no objections before settling on something secular.

The prelude

The organist plays softly for about twenty minutes before the ceremony is due to start. The pieces should be calm and peaceful, setting the mood for the event and leading up to the exciting moment when the bride arrives. Most organists will be able to suggest a repertoire, but suitable pieces include:

- 'Sheep may safely graze' by J.S. Bach
- Moonlight Sonata (slow movement); Pathétique Sonata (slow movement) by Beethoven
- Symphony no. 6 (slow movement) 'From the New World' by Dvořák
- 'Nimrod' from *Enigma Variations* by Elgar
- *Water Music*; Pastoral Symphony from *Messiah* by Handel
- 'Gymnopédie no. 1' by Satie.

The processional

Joyful and stately music is played as the bridal party enter the church and continues as they process down the aisle. The pace should be steady, making it easy to walk slowly without feeling rushed. You might like to choose one of the following:

- 'Trumpet Voluntary' by Boyce
- 'Theme from the St Anthony Chorale' by Brahms
- 'Trumpet Voluntary' ('Prince of Denmark's March') by Clarke
- 'Arrival of the Queen of Sheba'; 'Minuet' from *Music for the Royal Fireworks* by Handel
- 'Bridal March' by Parry
- 'Bridal March' from *Lohengrin* by Wagner.

Hymns and psalms

It is usual to have three hymns or psalms during the ceremony, the first at the beginning of the service, the second after the marriage and the third after you have signed the register. You can have just two hymns or only one if you prefer. It is advisable to choose hymns that are well known, especially if the congregation is small or you are not using a choir. Below is a selection of well-known popular hymns often used at weddings:

- 'Come down, O Love divine'
- 'Glorious things of thee are spoken'
- 'Jerusalem'
- 'Love divine, all loves excelling'
- 'Praise my soul the King of heaven'
- 'The Lord's my shepherd' (to the tune Crimond)
- 'Lord of all hopefulness'
- 'I vow to thee my country'
- 'Dear Lord and Father of mankind'.

Suitable psalms, which may be said or sung, include:

- Psalm 37 ('Put thou thy trust in the Lord . . .')
- Psalm 67 ('God be merciful unto us and bless us . . .')
- Psalm 83 ('How lovely is Thy dwelling place, O Lord of Hosts! . . .')
- Psalm 128 ('Blessed are all they that fear the Lord . . .').

Signing the register

At this point in the proceedings you might like a friend or relative to play a solo on a musical instrument or sing. Alternatively, the church choir could sing a psalm or anthem. Another option would be to book professional instrumentalists or singers to perform your favourite pieces or arrange for a recorded piece to be played. Whatever you would like to do, tell the minister which pieces you have chosen to be performed to ensure there is no objection. If you want to use recorded music, you need to obtain permission to set up a sound system; make sure you leave enough time to test it properly and enlist a competent operator. The same applies if you want to make a recording of the ceremony. You can choose from a wide range of classical, modern and popular instrumental arrangements and songs. Some of the most popular pieces include:

- 'Adagio in G Minor' (orchestral recording or organ) by Albinoni
- 'Jesu, joy of man's desiring' (organ with or without choir or soloist) by J.S. Bach
- 'Flower Duet' from *Lakmé* (soloists) by Delibes
- 'Ave Maria' (choir or soloist) by Gounod
- 'Ave Maria' (organ or strings, with or without choir or soloist) by Schubert
- 'Exultate Jubilate'; 'Laudate Dominum' (soloist) by Mozart.

The recessional

This is the moment for a really joyful explosion of sound, as the newly married couple and their attendants leave the church. Traditional choices include:

- Toccata in G by Dubois
- March no. 4 from *Pomp and Circumstance* by Elgar
- 'Wedding March' from *A Midsummer Night's Dream* by Mendelssohn
- Postlude in D by Smart
- Fanfare by Whitlock
- Toccata from *Symphony No. 5* by Widor.

Tip

Performances that take place at wedding ceremonies and receptions – whether live or of recorded music – are deemed 'private' so you do not need to pay any copyright fees or obtain a public broadcast licence.

Order of service sheets

When you have made a final decision on the music and readings for your ceremony you can have order of service sheets printed, or design them yourself on a computer, see pages 69–70. You will need to order one for each guest, plus a dozen extra. These should be placed at the church before the service, and it is the ushers' job to give one to each guest and to ensure that sheets are placed at the front of the church for the minister, bride and groom to use.

On the front of the service sheet the name of the church and the date and time of the ceremony appear in the centre of the page. The bride's name is printed in the bottom right-hand corner and the groom's in the bottom left-hand corner. Inside are printed all the verses of hymns, all the words of the prayers and responses, along with details of the music to be played. A printer will have a sample sheet on which you can base your layout, but you will need to provide a typed copy of the wording you want to use. Check this with the minister before going ahead with printing to ensure that all details are correct.

It is possible, though unlikely, that your chosen hymns will still be protected by copyright, in which case you will need to seek permission from the copyright holder to reprint the words in your order of service sheets. Details of this will be found in the hymn book, either in the acknowledgements at the front or under the paragraph on copyright. If permission is required, the relevant address will be shown in the hymn book. A few copyright holders ask for a reproduction fee, but most are happy with a brief printed acknowledgement.

Remember that you do not have to have printed order of service sheets. If you want to keep costs down you can use the service as laid out in a prayer book, and the congregation can sing from hymn books. Make sure that enough of these books are available for the ushers to distribute.

Bells

A glorious peal of bells enhances any traditional church ceremony. However, an increasing number of churches have only one bell, although they may be able to use a recorded peal. The bells can be rung before and after the ceremony, and the bellringers are paid in cash by the best man on the day. A peal of bells costs between £30 and £60.

Alice and Henry

Alice and Henry initially booked their wedding for 2.30pm, then changed the time to 2pm to fit in with their reception arrangements. Unfortunately the minister had made the change in his desk diary but had forgotten to make the change in the bellringers' book and the ringers turned up after the ceremony had started. Always double-check arrangements, especially if you make any changes.

Readings

Many people like to include one or two readings in their service, although this is not compulsory. Suitable readings from the Authorized Version of the Bible include:

- I Corinthians, Chapter 13 ('Love is patient and kind')
- Ecclesiastes 4, 9–12 ('Two are better than one')
- I John, Chapter 4, 7–12 ('Beloved, let us love one another')
- Ruth 1, 16–17 ('Whither thou goest, I will go')
- Song of Solomon 8, 6–7: ('Set me as a seal upon thine heart').

If you want a reading taken from any source other than the Bible, get your minister's agreement beforehand. There are many suitable poems that could be read, and more details are given on pages 129–30.

Civil ceremony

The key point to remember is that any music or reading included in a civil ceremony must be non-religious. For example, this means that you cannot have any version of 'Ave Maria' or 'Pie Jesu', or any extract from a mass or requiem, nor can you have readings from the Bible, the Koran, the Torah, or Gibran's 'The Prophet'. Many register offices will allow you to use your own music at the discretion of the superintendent registrar. Restrictions on space and the amount of time allowed for each wedding mean that you will almost certainly not be able to have live music, although you will probably be allowed to use your choice of recorded music for a few minutes before and after the ceremony.

Approved premises, such as castles and stately homes, will generally be more flexible, but do check before booking if music is very important to you, as some hotels and country houses have fairly strict policies about the use of music during the ceremony. At approved premises it is often possible to arrange the ceremony to include a prelude, processional and recessional (see pages 124–6) and you may be able to use live or recorded music.

As to your choice of music, any of the non-religious pieces listed on pages 124–6 would be suitable. You can get inspiration from the many compilations of romantic and mood music, both classical and modern, which are widely available on CD from record stores and libraries. Among the most popular modern pieces played at civil weddings are:

- 'Annie's Song' by John Denver
- 'The Miracle of Love' by the Eurythmics
- 'Your Song' by Elton John
- 'You've Got A Friend' by Carole King
- 'Love Me Tender' by Elvis Presley
- 'When A Man Loves A Woman' by Percy Sledge.

Readings

You may also be able to have one or more non-religious readings at a civil ceremony, again with the superintendent registrar's approval. These could be read by a family member or friend, or even by the bride or groom. Anthologies, such as *The Oxford Book of Marriage*, (Rubinstein, H (ed.), 1990, OUP), which is available from bookshops or libraries, are a useful source of suitable poems and prose. Suggestions include:

- 'If ever two were one, then surely we . . .' by Anne Bradstreet
- 'How do I love thee? Let me count the ways . . .' (from *Sonnets from the Portuguese*) by Elizabeth Barrett Browning
- 'Never marry but for love . . .' by William Penn
- 'My heart is like a singing bird . . .' (from *A Birthday*) by Christina Rossetti

- 'Shall I compare thee to a summer's day? . . .' ('Sonnet 18') by William Shakespeare
- 'My true love hath my heart and I have his. . .' (from *Arcadia*) by Sir Philip Sidney.

Alternative ceremonies

If you choose to have an alternative ceremony (i.e. one that carries no legal weight but which is a celebration of your marriage that takes place after a civil ceremony) you are free to choose any readings and music you wish, with or without religious content. See pages 28 and 151–3 for more information on the content of alternative ceremonies.

Music checklist

Name of musician(s)		
Address		
Telephone/fax/email		
Details of booking		
Cost		
Confirmed in writing		
	Name of piece of music	**Played by**
Prelude		
Processional		
Hymns		
Signing of the register		
Recessional		

Chapter 15

Wedding cake options

The traditional tiered wedding cake makes a grand centrepiece for the wedding feast and can take pride of place on a buffet table. At a sit-down meal the cake should be placed on a separate table where it can be seen by the guests but where it does not obscure their view of the bride and groom. Order the cake well in advance as traditional rich fruit cake improves with age and should be made at least two months before icing.

The first question to consider is how many people the cake will have to serve. Remember to allow for those absent on the day (either because they couldn't come or because you weren't able to invite them). You can send them a piece after the wedding in special little boxes (available in department stores); if you wish, these can be printed with details of your wedding.

No. portions needed	Shape	Size of tiers (allows for keeping top tier)
60	round, 2 tiers	25cm/10in, 15cm/6in
100	round, 3 tiers	28cm/11in, 18cm/7in, 12.5cm/5in
130–140	round, 3 tiers	30cm/12in, 20cm/8in, 15cm/6in
	square, 3 tiers	25cm/10in, 20cm/8in, 15cm/6in
160–180	round, 3 tiers	30cm/12in, 25cm/10in, 20cm/8in
	square, 3 tiers	28cm/11in, 23cm/9in, 18cm/7in
200–220	round, 4 tiers	30cm/12in, 25cm/10in, 20cm/8in, 15cm/6in
	square, 3 tiers	30cm/12in, 25cm/10in, 20cm/8in

Also decide whether you want to keep the top tier for a future celebration, such as your first wedding anniversary or the christening of your first child, and remember to allow for this in your calculations. You will need about 2.25kg/5lb of fruit cake for every 45 to 50 guests. Another way to estimate the size needed is by diameter of the cakes (see page 131).

Fruit cake, being very rich, is economical to serve as only small slices need be given. If you choose sponge cake instead you will get approximately half the number of servings per tier.

Using sponge cakes instead of fruit cakes

More and more people steer away from heavy fruit cakes, opting instead for vanilla or chocolate sponge. These cakes can be iced to look like a conventional cake, and if tiered, can be stacked or arranged using special pillars with interior rods, which go through the cake and rest on the stand beneath. These bear the weight of the cakes on top. Alternatively, sponge cakes can be frosted, or covered with rich ganache icing. However, if the weather is hot these finishes are likely to melt, so the cake must be displayed somewhere cool.

Tip

One way to keep costs down but still provide a spectacular centre-piece to the wedding meal is to have a cake which can double as dessert. A pyramid of chocolate-iced profiteroles, decorated with spun caramelised sugar, is ideal. Allow three buns per portion. You could also try a French croquembouche – a hillock of choux buns filled with flavoured creams, with caramel and spun sugar poured over – which is traditionally served at parties in France. A chocolate gâteau would be another good choice, or for a smaller gathering, a large Swiss roll, filled with cream and brandy-soaked glacé fruits, would look sumptuous and taste delicious.

Shapes and decorations

Square and round are the most popular shapes and can be arranged either on pillars or stacked, with the tiers resting on top of each other. Flower shapes are another possibility, or you could choose rectangles, octagons or horseshoes. White royal icing is the traditional choice, but fondant icing – being much softer – is easier to eat and gives you more scope for imaginative decoration as it can be moulded and modelled. Although white is the most common choice, the cake could be iced in a colour to fit in with the scheme of the flowers or bridesmaids' dresses.

The cake can be iced with swags, flowers, latticework or many other decorations. Professional confectioners will have a book of photographs showing all the different designs they offer. On top you can have a bride and groom model or a small arrangement of fresh flowers, which should be ordered with your other flowers. Silk flowers are a good alternative to fresh, or a skilled confectioner can make sugar flowers which can be kept as a souvenir. These add considerably to the cost, however, as they are very time-consuming to make.

Who will make the cake?

Making the cake yourself, or asking a family member or friend to do it, is a good way to save money. Ingredients for a simple three-tiered wedding cake (feeding 80–100 people) cost about £45 from a supermarket. Another way to keep costs down is to buy plain iced fruit cakes from a supermarket and construct your own tiered cake, which you can then have professionally decorated. Costs range from £10 to £30 per tier.

To make the cake yourself, start by baking it three months before the wedding. The tiers will probably have to be done in relays unless you have access to an extra-large oven. Once you have made the cakes, wrap them in greaseproof paper then in foil and store for at least two months in a cool, dry place until you are ready to ice them. Icing is a job best left to the professionals unless you are very experienced, and you should be able to take the cakes to a cake-decorator for icing and decoration four to six weeks before the wedding.

If you decide to have the cake made for you, consult the *Yellow Pages* for a suitable baker and confectioner. Shop around to compare prices and ask to taste a sample of a typical cake. Confirm all the details in writing when you order and remember to check:

- **when the cake will be delivered**
- **who will assemble it at the reception venue**. If you are using caterers they may do this or else the cake supplier will do it
- **how the cake will be packed**. Each tier should be boxed separately to avoid damage
- for a tiered cake, **whether the pillars and display tray are included in the price**
- if the top decorations are provided. Most confectioners will be able to offer you a wide choice
- **if the confectioner is insured against loss or damage of the cake prior to delivery or during transit**.

Tip

Storing the top layer is only possible if you choose a fruit cake, as sponge cakes do not keep for more than a few days. First you must strip off the icing, as this discolours if kept, and the marzipan, as this contains almond oil which turns rancid when stored. If it is likely that the cake will be used within the next year to 18 months, wrap it in plenty of acid-free tissue paper and store it in a cardboard box where the air can circulate round it. Do not keep it in an airtight tin or plastic box. Store in the coolest possible room, out of direct light. If it is likely that the cake is going to be kept for more than 18 months, wrap it in foil then put it into a double freezer bag and store it in the deep freeze, where it will keep well for up to two years.

Chapter 16

Photographs and video

As photographs and/or a video will be a lasting reminder of your wedding day, it is well worth hiring a professional for the occasion. In addition, you could ask one or two friends whom you know to be keen photographers to bring their cameras and take some extra shots – this way you will get some very personal and informal pictures as well. If you want to upload photographs on to a website or send them by email, or if you want to be able to edit photographs on your computer, you will need a digital camera (see page 71).

Personal recommendation is the best way to find a reliable photographer/video operator, but the *Yellow Pages* will supply many names, and you will probably be able to find one or two in your local high street. Bridal magazines are another good source, both of names of photographers/video operators and of ideas for different photographic styles.

Visit more than one and ask to see photographs/videos from several previous weddings. Make sure you are shown photographs/videos taken by the person you are planning to book, and not a compilation taken by several people. You will need to book about six months ahead of the wedding, possibly longer for a popular photographer/video operator.

Photographs

Decide what style of photography you would like:

- do you want very formal pictures?
- are you interested in having some very informal, candid shots?
- would you like some photographs to be posed in a more original and artistic way, perhaps at a venue away from the church and

reception such as a local park or riverside? Make sure your photographer is experienced at this type of work.

Your budget will dictate the number of photographs you ask for. A standard package usually contains 20 prints, starting with the groom's and best man's arrival at the church and ending at the reception when the cake is cut. You can add to this basic package as much as you like and can afford. The reportage style of wedding photography is very popular, and the finished album will tell the full story of the day, starting with the bride preparing to leave home and ending with the couple leaving the reception, with a mixture of traditional and informal photographs in between. However, you could pay £1,000 or more for this style of presentation, in a high-quality leather album.

Tip

Some couples use a professional photographer for the ceremony only and put a disposable flash camera on each table at the reception and ask the guests to take photographs. One of the brides-maids could collect all the cameras at the end of the day. Another idea, which takes a little more preparation but produces a wonderful informal souvenir, is to prepare album pages with mounts, then ask someone to take Polaroid shots of guests at each table, making sure everyone is included. The shots can then be mounted on the album pages, and guests asked to write a message underneath their picture.

Spend time talking to your photographer in advance of the day. You will need to consider the following points.

- **Does the photographer make you feel relaxed and do you think you can work happily with him or her on the day?** A good photographer must be helpful and unobtrusive but also needs to be able to manage people, persuade them to pose and make sure that the photography does not hold up the proceedings for too long.

- **How will the key shots be covered?** Are you in agreement with the photographer about the level of formality and the mixture of formal and informal photographs? Are there any special shots you want or any guest of whom you would like a close-up?
- **The photographer will need a timetable of the day and a list of the names of the most important guests who must be included.** You can also give a list of shots which you particularly want.
- Organising **group photographs** takes time, and your guests will not want to be kept waiting at the wedding venue for too long. One way of getting round this is to drop the traditional receiving line and have the group photographs taken at the reception venue while the guests are arriving and being given a drink. Tell the key people in advance that they will be wanted for group photographs at the start of the reception and make sure they know where to go when they arrive.
- **Check with your minister where and when photography is allowed in church.** Policies vary, and while some ministers are happy to have a few discreet photographs taken during the service – although not always of the marriage itself – others ask for no flash or stipulate a number of pictures allowed, and some will permit no photography in the church at all.

The photographer broke the rules

Marianna's vicar specified that only one picture could be taken during the signing of the register. However, her photographer chose to ignore this and slipped in several extra photographs, thus annoying the vicar and causing everyone to feel uncomfortable – a fact that inevitably showed up in the photographs. Tell your photographer what is allowed and make sure he or she knows that you are happy to go along with any rules laid down by the vicar.

Negotiating a package

Most estimates include an album containing a specified number of photographs. Some packages also include two smaller versions of the main album to be given to each of the sets of parents, and you can also select some photographs to be printed in a larger size for framing; these are charged for in addition to the basic package. Some photographers quote for the amount of time they spend at your wedding on the day and charge extra for prints; others charge for prints but not for their time, while some base the cost on their time and offer unlimited prints.

Check for hidden extras such as development, VAT and delivery of proofs. If you want any special effects such as hand-tinting, sepia or black-and-white photographs, specify these when you make your booking and get confirmation of the cost. The photographer should send you a proof set of all the photographs taken about a week after the wedding, and you can choose the ones you would like included in your album. You can also circulate the proofs round any others who might like to buy prints.

Popular wedding-day photographs

The list below covers most of the usual wedding photographs, but you will probably not want to have all of them.

Before the ceremony

- Bride and bridesmaids at home, preparing for the ceremony
- Close-up of bride before wedding
- Bride and father before leaving home
- Guests arriving at wedding venue
- Groom and best man at wedding venue before the ceremony
- Ushers at the wedding venue
- Bridesmaids and bride's mother arriving at wedding venue
- Bride and father arriving at wedding venue

In the church (if permitted)

- Bride's procession down the aisle
- The marriage ceremony (if permitted)
- Exchange of rings
- Signing of the register
- Musicians performing
- Bride and groom walking back down the aisle
- Bride and groom emerging from church

After the ceremony

- Bride and groom together
- Couple with bridesmaids and/or pages
- Couple with best man, bridesmaids and/or pages
- Bridesmaids and pages
- Couple with bride's parents
- Couple with groom's parents
- Couple with both sets of parents
- Couple with all family members of both sides
- Couple with all friends
- Entire wedding party
- Guests throwing confetti
- Couple leaving for reception

At a register office/approved venue

Check whether there are any restrictions on where you can have photographs taken inside the venue.

At the reception

- Receiving line
- Informal photographs during reception
- Top table
- Each side table
- Speeches: bride's father, groom, best man
- Cutting the cake
- First dance (bride and groom)
- Bride throwing bouquet
- Couple leaving reception

Other shots

- Portrait of bride
- Portrait of groom
- Close-up of ring(s) on finger
- Other special requests

Insurance

Ensure that your photographer is covered by a professional indemnity, which covers camera problems and lost or damaged film. Insurance cannot cover points of style, so if the photographs are not what you wanted or hoped for you will have to seek compensation from the photographer direct. If you take out wedding insurance (see Chapter 21), most policies cover you for the cost of a retake if the photographer does not show up on the day or the films or negatives are lost or damaged.

Photography checklist

Name of photographer	
Address	
Telephone/fax	
Contact	
Date booked	
Confirmed in writing	
Agreed fee	
What is included in the package?	
Time of photographer's arrival at bride's home/wedding venue	
Time of photographer's departure from the reception	
Date proofs will be supplied	
Special effects requested	

Video

More and more people are having professional videos made of their wedding day. It is tempting to ask a friend who owns a camcorder or is willing to hire one to do this for you, and you will certainly make a big saving. However, producing a well-shot, watchable video takes some skill, and you need to be certain that your friend is up to the task and is happy to concentrate on filming rather than entering into the fun of the occasion. Of course, if you are not worried about the occasional wobble or muffled sound, then an amateur video is worth considering. Digital camcorders give better results (see page 73).

Tips for making an amateur video

- Well in advance, draw up a list of shots that should definitely be included. You can shadow the official photographer and take some film from the sidelines as the main shots are set up – but do not get in the way.
- Remember to take a spare battery and plenty of video tape.
- Visit the church and reception venue ahead of the day if possible and work out the best positions for your shots. Check the position of useful power sockets.
- If you use a separate microphone, which will give good sound quality during the ceremony and speeches, position it where guests are unlikely to brush against it or knock it over.
- Use a hand-held microphone and ask guests to speak directly to the camera.
- Take as many shots as you can of people smiling and laughing.
- You will get a much better finished result if you can get access to editing equipment, so that shots can be shortened or intercut.
- Use shots of the church/wedding venue interior, or close-ups of floral arrangements or the bridal bouquet, to intersperse with the action shots.
- Be on the lookout for unusual or amusing shots.
- Keep the camera steady, using a tripod when necessary.
- Each sequence should be fairly short, otherwise the finished film will run for hours.
- Be sparing with your use of the zoom lens.
- Bookshops and libraries have a wide stock of books with detailed information on making a successful amateur video.

If you decide to hire a professional, you should follow the same selection procedure as for a photographer. Styles of video vary, so look at a few samples to find the type that best suits you. Any reputable video service will provide insurance, and some also offer a customer dissatisfaction clause. With this, financial compensation may be available if an independent arbitration panel judges the final product to be of an inferior standard to that agreed in your contract.

As with photography, you should be able to agree on a package deal, which will include a specified number of copies of the video and will stipulate at what stage the filming will start and finish. Check with your minister that he or she does not object to a video being made of the ceremony. (You will probably have to pay the church a small fee for having a video of the ceremony.) Remember that to achieve the best effects the video company may have to set up microphones and extra lighting.

Video checklist

Name of video company	
Address	
Telephone/fax	
Contact	
Date booked	
Confirmed in writing	
Agreed fee	
What is included in the package?	
Time of video operator's arrival at bride's home/wedding venue	
Time of video operator's departure from the reception	
When will the video be delivered?	

Chapter 17

Civil ceremonies

For many years the proportion of civil to religious marriages was roughly equal, but since the introduction of the 1994 law permitting non-religious weddings to take place at premises other than register offices, the number of civil marriages has been steadily increasing, until currently 62 per cent of all weddings are civil. Although most of these still take place at register offices, an increasing number of couples each year choose to marry in alternative licensed premises and this number looks likely to rise as more and more venues apply for licences, thus widening the choice. For more information about approved premises see Chapter 2, page 21.

Whether you choose to hold your civil ceremony in a register office or elsewhere, you will have to satisfy various legal criteria before you can marry (see Appendix).

The wedding day

The arrangements and timings for a civil wedding will vary considerably, depending on whether you have chosen to have a very quiet register office ceremony, a grand-scale wedding with all the trimmings at approved premises, or something in between. The two case histories on pages 146–151, give some idea of what is involved at either end of the spectrum.

You can arrive at the wedding venue together or separately. Remember that register offices allow a fairly brief period for each wedding, so time your arrival for about ten minutes before the ceremony is due to begin. At approved premises the reception is sometimes held at the same venue as the ceremony, so there is unlikely to be more than one wedding on the same day. You can have a best man and bridesmaids if you wish, but all that the law requires is two adult witnesses, who can be family members or friends.

Before the register office ceremony, you and your guests will gather in an ante-room. Wherever the marriage takes place, the couple will have a brief private interview with the superintendent registrar before the ceremony, in which all details are checked for accuracy and the attendance fee is collected. The couple and guests then assemble in the room where the marriage is to be held.

The civil ceremony

Certain parts of the ceremony are obligatory, but in places you can choose from a variety of wordings, as indicated below. At most register offices the superintendent registrar offers a choice of additional wordings to embellish the ceremony which you can incorporate if you wish, and you may also be able to add some words of your own.

The ceremony begins with the superintendent registrar saying: *'This place in which you are now met has been duly sanctioned according to the law for the celebration of marriages. You are here to witness the joining in matrimony of (man's full name) and (woman's full name). If any person present knows of any lawful impediment to this marriage, he should declare it now.'*

The superintendent registrar asks the couple to stand. The guests remain seated. The superintendent registrar confirms the couple's full names and then says to them: *'Before you are joined in matrimony I have to remind you of the solemn and binding character of the ceremony of marriage. Marriage according to the law of this country is the union of one man with one woman, voluntarily entered into for life, to the exclusion of all others. Now I am going to ask each of you in turn to declare that you do not know of any lawful reason why you should not be married to each other.'*

The couple in turn then repeat, either: *'I do solemnly declare that I know not of any lawful impediment why I, (full name), may not be joined in matrimony to (full name).'*

or

'I declare that I know of no legal reason why I, (full name), should not be joined in marriage to (full name).'

or

In response to the question: *'Are you, (full name), free lawfully to marry (full name)?'* respond, *'I am'*.

The superintendent registrar then says to all those present: *'Now the solemn moment has come for these two persons to contract the marriage before you, their witnesses. Will you all please stand.'*

In turn, the man and then the woman take their partner by the hand and repeat either: *'I call upon these persons here present to witness that I, (full name), do take thee, (full name) to be my lawful wedded wife/husband.'*

or

'I (full name) take you (or thee) (full name) to be my wedded wife/husband.'

There is no legal obligation to give or exchange a wedding ring or rings. If you do use rings, you will be asked to take the ring and place it on the other's ring finger and hold it there. This is the point in the ceremony where you may be allowed to personalise your vows if you wish. Alternatively, the superintendent registrar may be able to suggest different forms of words, such as: *'I give/accept this ring as a token of our marriage.'*

or

'Receive this ring as a token of my love and our marriage, a symbol of all that we have promised and all that we now share.'

Then the superintendent registrar says: *'(Full name) and (full name), you have both made the declarations prescribed by law, and have made a solemn and binding contract with each other, in the presence of the witnesses here assembled. You are now husband and wife together.'*

After a pause, where the couple may kiss each other and be congratulated by the guests, the superintendent registrar says: *'Will you now all please be seated while the register is signed.'*

The register is signed by the couple, two witnesses, the registrar and the superintendent registrar. A copy is written on to a marriage certificate which is given to the couple.

Personalising a civil ceremony

In addition to the words printed above – which must be included by law – you may be able to add personal touches to a civil ceremony in the form of non-religious music, poetry, readings or vows (see Chapter 14). However, you must discuss any additions with the superintendent registrar when booking the wedding. Some will allow only minor inclusions, regardless of whether you are marrying in a register office or approved premises, while others are happy to allow you more freedom. Whatever you want to add, *the content must be strictly non-religious*, and you should check first with the superintendent registrar that any material you want to use is permissible.

At approved premises, which are often booked for the ceremony and reception, thus allowing you more time, you may be able to organise a longer, more formal ceremony, possibly including a processional and recessional and the inclusion of more music. Do not take this for granted however, and check before making any arrangements, as some approved premises prefer to keep the ceremony brief and simple.

Leaving the civil ceremony

At approved premises you will probably be having the reception at the same venue, and will have already discussed where best to take photographs.

For a register office wedding, you should be able to spend some time outside posing for photographs, although depending on where the office is sited you may prefer to have photographs taken elsewhere. On a busy day the next wedding party will be arriving soon after your ceremony is over, so bear this in mind when briefing a photographer, if you use one.

In either setting, find out what the policy is on confetti.

Case history

A small wedding at a register office

Kate and Rod wanted a wedding that was special, but with minimal fuss and low expense. Organisation went on over five months, and the ceremony was held at the local register office, followed by lunch at a hotel. Three months later the couple held a party for a wider group of friends.

Guests and gifts
Rod designed and produced the invitations on his computer. Twenty-five guests, including one child, came to the ceremony and lunch. As wedding presents, Kate and Rod asked for gift vouchers from two specified shops. Eighty people came to the party, and the invitations made it clear that this was a 'don't-bring-a-present' event.

On the wedding day
Guests parked at the hotel where the reception was to be held, and walked to the nearby register office. Kate, who wore a pale blue suit and navy hat and carried a bouquet, arrived first with her family, while Rod, who hired a black lounge suit, came along later.

The ceremony
The couple had made a tape of two French waltzes, a stately one, which was played as everyone entered, and a more lively tune, composed and recorded by friends, which was played during the signing of the register. Two poems were read by guests, *The Confirmation* by Edwin Muir after the initial vows, and *The Frog Prince* by Stevie Smith at the end. The registrar checked both poems before the ceremony to ensure that they had no religious content and were not flippant.

Photography
A professional photographer took just 12 shots, some at the register office and some at the hotel where the lunch was held.

The reception
After drinking sparkling wine provided by the hotel, chatting, having formal and informal photographs taken in the hotel gardens, the wedding party sat down to a three-course lunch. Kate and Rod provided their own wine to go with the meal, and the hotel charged £5 per bottle corkage. Tables were decorated with small posies. There were no formal speeches, just a couple of toasts with champagne,

again provided by the hotel. The single-tier fruit cake was bought from a local shop and iced professionally in a simple design.

After lunch, the wedding party went to Kate and Rod's house, where friends helped by serving tea and, later, by driving the couple the 30 miles to a B&B on the coast, where they had a three-night stay. The couple took their main honeymoon, in Crete, three months later, immediately after the party.

The party

Three months after the wedding, Kate and Rod held a party to which they invited family and a wide circle of friends. A friend arranged the hire of a hall at a discount and a buffet was supplied by a local caterer, although the couple over-estimated and ordered too much food. The couple provided a small amount of drink, asked friends to bring a bottle, and also had a pay-bar, although hardly any of the guests made use of this. A band played ceilidh music and there was a toast, speeches and another cake.

Timings

On the day:

11.00	Leave home, drive to hotel and park car. Walk to register office, arrive 11.15.
11.30	Wedding ceremony and photographs.
12.10	Walk back to hotel for reception.
12.30-1.45	Wine, chat and photographs.
1.45	Lunch.
8.00	Driven to honeymoon B&B.

What it cost

The wedding day

Ceremony and certificate	£61.50
Kate's outfit	£340.00
Hire of Rod's outfit	£30.00
Bouquet/buttonhole	£78.50
Photographer: 12 shots, plus album	£150.00
Reception: hotel bill (including lunch for 26, drinks, corkage and VAT)	£821.00

Cake	£40.00
Wine	£150.00
Total	*£1,671.00*

The party	
Hire of hall and cash bar	
(with discount via friend)	£50.00
Band	£250.00
Buffet	£500.00
Spanish sparkling wine for toasts	£60.00
Cake	£56.00
Total (not including honeymoon)	*£916.00*

Case history
A family wedding at approved licensed premises

Chloe and Monty spent ten months planning their wedding. The organisation was very time-consuming, as both were living and working in London, but the wedding was taking place near their home town, about 80 miles away, and they made numerous trips to order flowers, buy the dress, fix the reception details and so on.

Both ceremony and reception were held in the Council Chamber of the Town Hall, a large room beautifully decorated with pictures and velvet hangings.

Guests and gifts
Invitations were ordered from a department store. There were 88 guests, including seven children. The couple asked for gift vouchers, and were also given money and other presents.

On the day
Chloe arrived in a gold Jaguar, belonging to and driven by a friend. She wore a classic ivory satin wedding dress and tiara, and was attended by two bridesmaids and a page, who wore outfits from chain-store wedding collections. Bride and bridesmaids carried posies, and buttonholes were provided for all the guests. Monty hired a blue velvet Mozart-style jacket and navy trousers, plus a gold brocade waistcoat and cravat.

The ceremony

The live music was provided mainly by friends and family. A brass quartet played the Minuet from Handel's *Water Music* at the entrance of the bride and La Rejouissance from Handel's *Music for the Royal Fireworks* for the recession. The groom's brother, accompanied by a hired harpist, sang three traditional folk songs during the ceremony, *The Lark in the Clear Air, I will Give my Love an Apple* and *My Love's an Arbutus*. The groom's sister read a poem, *I Will Be Here* by Steven Curtis Chapman, and his grandmother read a Celtic blessing, *May Peace Guard the Door of Your House*. The bride's father gave her away. The couple wrote their own vows.

Photography

A professional photographer took over 200 shots before and after the ceremony, from which the couple chose 30 to make up an album. The bride's brother took video film of the whole day. Taking the photographs took longer than anticipated, which had a knock-on effect on timings for the rest of the day, but fortunately the venue was flexible and allowed the wedding party to continue for an extra half-hour, until 11.30pm.

The reception

Once the photography was over, guests were served buck's fizz and had a chance to sit down and chat. The couple had intended to have a receiving line, but abandoned the idea, because everyone had already had a chance to meet and time was running short. A sit-down three-course meal, provided by caterers and served by waitresses, followed accompanied by wines bought by the couple. The caterers did not charge corkage. One of the catering team acted as informal master of ceremonies, and introduced the speeches, toasts and the cutting of the cake. After the meal a four-piece folk band plus caller played for a barn dance which ended at 11.30pm. During this time a pay-bar was available, and in the middle of the evening bread, cheese, pâté and soft drinks were served. The couple stayed the night at a local hotel, and left next morning for a ten-day honeymoon in Italy.

Timings

On the day:

2.30	Bride arrives, sees registrar.
2.40–3.00	Ceremony with music.
3.15–4.30	Photographs.
4.30–5.30	Buck's fizz, sit down and chat.
5.30	Wedding breakfast served.
8.00	Meal ends, band set up.
8.30–11.30	Barn dance.

What it cost

Hire of venue, ceremony and certificate	1,029.00
Chloe's outfit	450.00
Make-up lesson and make-up	150.00
Hairdresser	50.00
Hire of Monty's outfit	206.00
Attendants' outfits	220.00
Flowers	389.00
Hire of harpist and trombonist	130.00
Photographer: 30 shots plus album	345.00
Reception food: sit-down meal, plus evening refreshments	1,600.00
Drinks: wine, champagne and soft drinks, all bought by the couple	347.00
Licence for evening bar	50.00
Cake	113.00
Band	400.00
Thank-you gifts	200.00
Insurance	50.00
Stationery	110.00
Total (not including honeymoon)	£5,839.00

Alternative ceremonies

Although not legally binding, an alternative ceremony can make an excellent follow-on from a civil marriage and enables you to have exactly the sort of ceremony you would like. You could create your own ceremony and write your own vows, which need not follow a particular set of beliefs but which can, if you wish, include religious elements.

A humanist ceremony

Humanists do not believe in any god, an afterlife or the super-natural. Their beliefs are founded on the idea that people should try to live full and happy lives and in doing this, make it easier for other people to do the same. A humanist wedding ceremony embodies these ideas and can be tailored to fit your wishes and personalities.

Suresh and Ruth

Suresh, who is Indian, and Ruth, who is English, had differing views from their parents regarding their wedding ceremony. Their parents felt that the religious element was important, although this would create difficul-ties because of the difference in cultures and expectations. Suresh and Ruth wanted a non-religious event. So they chose to have a humanist cer-emony, which they wrote themselves, straight after their civil marriage. They wanted a ceremony where they could have control over the words they used and the content. The humanist ceremony accorded with their belief that people should have freedom of choice in the main decisions of life, and should be able to celebrate one of the principal milestones of their lives in a non-religious way. The ceremony gave them the opportu-nity to make a serious public commitment to share their lives, despite the cultural and racial differences in their backgrounds, in a setting that both found poignant, moving and very pertinent to each of them as individuals and as a couple.

A humanist celebrant, with whom they had met beforehand to discuss the content of the ceremony, conducted it for them. In his introduction, the celebrant said: '*Ruth and Suresh recognise the uniqueness of their marriage, which crosses cultural and racial boundaries. It is very impor-tant to them that everyone, whatever his or her beliefs, feels comfortable about the proceedings and respects the decisions they have made. Above all they want friends and relatives to be a part of their day and wit-ness their commitment to each other.*'

Brothers of the bride and groom each gave a reading, then the couple repeated marriage vows similar to those used in a church service but without any mention of God. They exchanged rings, and music was played while they signed a register. The proceedings concluded with the bride's sister reading from an American Indian ceremony: '*Now you will feel no rain, for each of you will be shelter for the other. Now you will feel no cold, for each of you will be warmth to the other. Now there is no more loneliness. Now you are two persons, but there is only one life before you. Go now to your dwelling to enter into the days of your life together. And may your days be good and long upon the earth.*'

You can choose from a wide selection of poetry and readings, and whichever type of music you like to enhance the proceedings. Contact the British Humanist Association★ for more details.

If you are considering having a humanist ceremony it is a good idea to explain in advance to your guests, perhaps in an explanatory note sent out with the invitations, exactly who humanists are and what they believe. You should also remember that such a ceremony may not be entirely acceptable to others, such as your parents, particularly if they would prefer you to have a ceremony that meets their own religious beliefs.

Chapter 18

Religious ceremonies

Most religious ceremonies follow a set traditional procedure, which you can discuss with the minister when you make the initial arrangements. You will have to satisfy various legal criteria before you will be permitted to have any sort of religious ceremony (see the Appendix).

Church of England marriage ceremony

When you first visit the minister who will conduct your marriage he or she will tell you about the procedure for arranging the wedding, publishing the banns and organising the ceremony itself. Details of the documents you need to produce at this meeting are given on page 219. At this first meeting you can set the date and time of the wedding and discuss details such as who will play the organ, whether you want to use the church choir, your choice of music and where you can put flowers. You can also book a date and time for a rehearsal if your wedding is not too far in the future.

The minister will want to discuss the religious significance of the marriage service with you, so you may be asked to attend a series of marriage preparation sessions, during which the ceremony will be explained in detail and you will have the opportunity to think through the implications of marriage. The ceremonies of the Church of Scotland*, Church in Wales and Church of Ireland are very similar to that of the Church of England. See pages 32–3 for details of the Church of England ceremony of blessing for second marriages.

Catherine and Alistair

Catherine and Alistair got married by special licence (see page 221) because neither of them lived in the parish of the church in which they were planning to marry. 'The vicar gave us the impression that he would arrange the licence but he went on holiday without having done so, and the deaconess who took over assumed that we had made the arrangements ourselves. Five days before the wedding we realised that we didn't have the licence, and my fiancé had to visit Lambeth Palace to sort it out. It was a close-run thing, and a better discussion, with proper clarification over who was responsible for what, would have avoided it.'

Order of service

You will need to discuss the order of the service and which version of the ceremony you would like to use (see below). The service usually begins with a few words of introduction and a hymn, followed by the marriage itself. After the marriage has taken place there may be prayers, further hymns and possibly an address and some readings before the register is signed. For more information on choosing music and readings, see Chapter 14. Once you have worked out the exact order and decided on the music and readings, you can draw up an order of service for printing (see page 127).

Versions of the marriage service

There are three current versions of the marriage service to choose from. The versions dating from 1966 and 2000 are available as inexpensive booklets from Church House Bookshop at the General Synod of the Church of England★, so it is possible to study them in detail before deciding which version you would like to use.

- The version from the **1662 Book of Common Prayer** – The language is old-fashioned, and the bride's promise to obey her husband is an obligatory part of the service. It is not used very frequently but it is sometimes chosen by couples who like the older, more formal language and want a very traditional ceremony.
- **The form of Solemnisation of Matrimony 1966** – The language is similar in style to that of the 1662 version, but the bride's

promise to obey and serve her husband is optional, and the language of the introduction is more moderate.

- **The 2000 Marriage Service (Common Worship)** — The language is modern and direct. Again, the bride can choose whether or not she wants to promise to obey, and the couple can decide whether or not they want the possible future birth of children to be mentioned.

In the details of the ceremony given below, wordings are given from the 1966 and 2000 versions for comparison.

The ceremony

- Before the service starts the organist plays gentle music to create the right mood in the church. When the bride arrives the organist plays the music for the processional, and the groom and best man stand and move to the head of the aisle. The congregation then rises.
- The bride holds her father's right arm and, followed by the bridesmaids and pages, walks slowly down the aisle. The chief bridesmaid walks directly behind the bride, followed by the other attendants.
- The groom and best man may turn to greet the bride as she walks down the aisle or at the chancel steps.
- At the chancel steps the bride lifts back her veil if she is wearing one, perhaps helped by the chief bridesmaid. She hands her bouquet to the chief bridesmaid, who keeps it until the register has been signed.

The marriage

The minister greets the bridal party and congregation with a few introductory words and then begins the ceremony, which lasts about half an hour, depending on how many hymns and readings you are adding (with three hymns, two readings and an address, the service will take about 50 minutes). The congregation remain standing for the marriage itself and the hymns but may sit for the address and sit or kneel during the prayers. These moves can either be included in an order of service sheet, or the minister will tell the congregation what to do.

The service begins with a few words on the significance of marriage and its purposes:

1966: *'Dearly beloved, we are gathered here in the sight of God and in the face of this congregation, to join together this man and this woman in Holy Matrimony; which is an honourable estate, instituted of God himself, signifying unto us the mystical union that is betwixt Christ and his Church . . .'*

2000: *'In the presence of God, Father, Son and Holy Spirit, we have come together to witness the marriage of N. (groom) and N. (bride), to pray for God's blessing on them, to share their joy and to celebrate their love. Marriage is a gift of God in creation through which husband and wife may know the grace of God. It is given that as man and woman grow together in love and trust, they shall be united with one another in heart, body and mind, as Christ is united with his bride, the Church. The gift of marriage brings husband and wife together in the delight and tenderness of sexual union and joyful commitment to the end of their lives. It is given as the foundation of family life in which children are [born and] nurtured and in which each member of the family, in good times and bad, may find strength, companionship and comfort, and grow to maturity in love . . .'*

The minister then asks whether any member of the congregation knows of any reason why the couple should not be married:

1966: *'Therefore if any man can shew any just cause, why they may not lawfully be joined together, let him now speak, or else hereafter for ever hold his peace.'*

2000: *'First, I am required to ask anyone present who knows a reason why these persons may not lawfully marry, to declare it now.'*

The minister then asks the couple if either knows of any reason why they should not marry.

1966: *'I require and charge you both, as ye will answer at the dreadful day of judgement when the secrets of all hearts be disclosed, that if either of you know any impediment, why ye may not be lawfully joined together in Matrimony, ye do confess it. For be ye well assured, that so many as are coupled together otherwise than God's word doth allow are not joined together by God; neither is their Matrimony lawful.'*

2000: *'The vows you are about to take are to be made in the presence of God, who is judge of all and who knows all the secrets of our hearts; therefore if either of you knows a reason why you may not lawfully marry, you must declare it now.'*

The couple are then asked in turn if each will marry the other:

1966: *'N. Wilt thou have this woman to thy wedded wife, to live together according to God's law in the holy estate of Matrimony? Wilt thou love her, comfort her, honour and keep her, in sickness and in health? And, forsaking all other, keep thee only unto her, so long as ye both shall live?'*

2000: *'N., will you take N. to be your husband? Will you love him, comfort him, honour and protect him, and, forsaking all others, be faithful to him as long as you both shall live?'*

The bride and groom respond, *'I will'*.

1966: The minister asks who gives the woman to be married. The bride's father takes the bride's right hand and gives it to the minister who places it in the groom's right hand. This concludes the bride's father's role in the ceremony, and he steps back and joins the bride's mother in the front pew. Some couples prefer to omit this part of the ceremony.

2000: After the bride has responded, *'I will'*, the minister says to the congregration, *'Will you, the families and friends of N. and N., support and uphold them in their marriage now and in the years to come?'* The congregation responds: *'We will.'*

In this ceremony, the giving away of the bride by her father is also optional, but may be performed at this stage, as in the 1966 version. Alternatively, the minister may say to the parents of both bride and groom: *'N. and N. have declared their intention towards each other. As their parents, will you now entrust your son and daughter to one another as they come to be married?'* The parents respond, *'We will.'*

Next the couple make their wedding vows, taking it in turn to repeat the words after the minister:

1966: *'I N. take thee N. to my wedded wife, to have and to hold from this day forward, for better, for worse; for richer, for poorer; in sickness and in health; to love and to cherish till death us do part, according to God's holy law; and thereto I give thee my troth.'* (Women have the option to obey in this service.)

2000: *'I, N., take you, N., to be my husband, to have and to hold from this day forward; for better, for worse, for richer, for poorer, in sickness and in health, to love and to cherish (or, to love, cherish, and obey), till death us do part, according to God's holy law. In the presence of God I make this vow.'*

Some couples choose to learn their vows off by heart so they can say them to each other without needing to be prompted by the minister.

The best man places the ring(s) on an open prayer book, which the minister offers him. The rings are blessed, then the minister gives the bride's ring to the groom, who places it on her finger and repeats the words:

1966: *'With this ring I thee wed; with my body I thee honour; and all my worldly goods with thee I share: In the name of the Father, and of the Son, and of the Holy Ghost. Amen.'*

2000: *'I give you this ring as a sign of our marriage. With my body I honour you, all that I am I give to you, and all that I have I share with you, within the love of God, Father, Son, and Holy Spirit.'*

If rings are exchanged these words are also repeated by the bride as she places a ring on the groom's finger. The minister then pronounces the couple husband and wife:

1966: *'Those whom God hath joined together let no man put asunder . . . I pronounce that they be man and wife together, In the name of the Father, and of the Son, and of the Holy Ghost. Amen.'*

2000: *'I therefore proclaim that they are husband and wife. Those whom God has joined together let no one put asunder.'*

The ceremony continues with prayers, hymns, readings and/or an address. If the service includes communion or mass it will take place at this point. The service ends with the signing of the register.

Seating plan during the marriage

	ALTAR		
	Minister		
Bride's father	BRIDE	GROOM	Best Man
	Chief Bridesmaid		
	Attendants		
Bride's mother		Groom's parents	
Bride's close family		Groom's close family	
Other members of bride's family		Other members of groom's family	
Friends		Friends	

Signing the register

The bride and groom, chief bridesmaid and best man, other attendants, bride's and groom's parents and minister are all present at the signing of the register. This can either take place in the vestry (in which case the bridal party gain a few minutes of privacy in which they can relax a little before leaving church) or at a side table, in view of the congregation. Music is usually played or sung while the congregation wait for the register to be signed.

The marriage register is signed by the minister, the bride, using her maiden name, the groom and two adult witnesses – perhaps the two fathers or the two mothers or the best man and chief bridesmaid. Decide before the ceremony who will sign. The marriage certificate, which is a copy of the register entry, is given to the couple by the minister (although the best man will usually take charge of it during the day).

After the register has been signed, the bridal party and congregation leave the church. The chief bridesmaid returns the bride's bouquet to her and arranges her train. The bride takes her husband's left arm, the organist begins the recessional music and the bridal party leaves the church in the following order: bride and groom, chief bridesmaid and best man, other attendants, bride's mother with groom's father, and groom's mother with bride's father. The congregation follow, with those seated at the front of the church leaving before those seated at the back.

Outside the church

Once outside the church photographs are taken.

- The congregation may shower the couple with confetti if allowed by the minister. Alternatives to confetti are rice, which can sting but may be cleared up for you by the birds, or flower petals which could be provided in baskets by bridesmaids.
- The best man helps the photographer to marshal the guests into groups for the photographs.
- The best man or ushers should check inside the church to make sure that nothing has been left behind, including top hats and gloves belonging to the bridal party, cameras and umbrellas.

- When the photographs have all been taken, the bride and groom leave the church for the reception. Next to leave are the couple's parents and the bridesmaids and pages. Guests follow on, and it is up to the best man to make sure that everyone has the means to get to the reception. He should be last to leave the church but must also try not to arrive too late at the reception, where he may be wanted to take part in the receiving line.

Roman Catholic ceremony

The Roman Catholic ceremony can be conducted with or without a nuptial mass (a wedding without nuptial mass is usually celebrated when one partner is non-Christian). The minister is normally a priest, but if the ceremony is without a mass, he may be a deacon. The ceremony is similar to that of the Church of England and begins with a welcome, an introduction, and Bible readings but has a responsorial psalm. After the minister's address comes the marriage rite:

The minister then says: *'You have come together in this church so that the Lord may seal and strengthen your love in the presence of the Church's minister and this community. Christ abundantly blesses this love. He has already consecrated you in baptism and now he enriches and strengthens you by a special sacrament so that you may assume the duties of marriage in mutual and lasting fidelity. And so, in the presence of this Church, I ask you to state your intentions.*

'I shall now ask you if you freely undertake the obligations of marriage, and to state that there is no legal impediment to your marriage.'

He then asks the couple three questions to which they respond in turn after each question *'I am'*:

'Are you ready freely and without reservation to give yourselves to each other in marriage?'

'Are you ready to love and honour each other as man and wife for the rest of your lives?'

'Are you ready to accept children lovingly from God, and bring them up according to the law of Christ and his Church?'

Finally, the couple take their vows with words similar to those in the Church of England ceremony. The bride does not promise to obey.

Minister: *'You have declared your consent before the Church. May the Lord in his goodness strengthen your consent and fill you both with his blessings. What God has joined together, let no man put asunder.'*

The rings are then blessed and given with the words:
'May the Lord bless this ring (these rings) which you give (to each other) as the sign of your love and fidelity.'

The couple in turn then say:
'N. (Christian name only) take this ring as a sign of my love and fidelity. In the name of the Father, and of the Son, and of the Holy Spirit.'

If the marriage ceremony is taking place within a mass, the mass continues after the exchange of rings. A nuptial blessing is given by the minister before communion in a nuptial mass, or after the intercessions in a ceremony without mass. The signing of the register follows the final prayers and hymn, and the couple then leave church together.

Non-conformist or free church ceremonies

Marriages which take place in churches such as Methodist, Baptist and United Reformed Church use a ceremony very similar to that of the Church of England. The order of service may be slightly altered.

Quaker ceremony

Marriages take place in a specially appointed 'meeting for worship' which mainly follows the usual simple Quaker practice of prayerful silence, with an opportunity for those present to offer their own blessings and good wishes. Local Quakers would hope to offer ongoing support to any couple 'married in the care of the meeting', and therefore expect a couple to have some involvement in the Quaker community, with one probably in membership, or strongly in sympathy with Quaker principles. Ample time should therefore be allowed for consulting the registering officer.

An explanation of the procedure is given, the couple then stand and make their declaration of marriage using these words: *'Friends, I take this my friend, (full name), to be my husband/wife, promising, through Divine assistance (or, with God's help), to be unto him/her a loving and faithful wife/husband, so long as we both on earth shall live.'*

Wedding rings are not formally exchanged during a Quaker wedding, but the couple may like to give each other a ring after making their declarations. They sign the Quaker marriage certificate in front of the first two witnesses and the certificate is read aloud by the registering officer, either immediately or towards the end of the meeting.

A period of silence then follows during which anyone present may speak, perhaps to pray, or offer their loving support. At the end of the meeting the couple and the registering officer sign the civil register; afterwards all those present sign the Quaker marriage certificate, as witnesses also.

Jewish ceremony

The wedding usually takes place in a synagogue, but other venues such as halls or hotel suites are also acceptable. A quorum or *minyan* of at least ten adult males for an orthodox service, or ten adult men and women for a non-orthodox service, should be present. Prior to the ceremony, the groom approaches the bride and lowers her veil over her face. Who accompanies the groom and bride to the flower-decorated wedding canopy or *chuppah* varies according to custom. Sometimes the groom may be escorted by his father and the bride's father, or by his parents; while the bride is escorted by the two mothers, or by her parents. Most often these days the bride is accompanied by her father to meet the groom. The bride can, if she so wishes, walk round the groom three or seven times, depending on custom, before standing on his right. While this is happening the rabbi or cantor chants a welcome blessing.

The ceremony itself begins with the rabbi reciting a blessing over a goblet of wine from which the bride and groom then drink. The groom places the wedding ring on the forefinger of the bride's right hand, saying '*Behold you are wedded to me with this ring according to the Law of Moses and Israel.*' (The bride may transfer the ring to her left hand after the ceremony.) The *ketubah* or marriage contract, which is written in Aramaic, has already been signed by the witnesses prior to the ceremony. The bride and groom do not have to sign the *ketubah* to make it valid in Jewish law, but may, if they wish, sign the abstract printed on the reverse side. The *ketubah* is read aloud, and the seven benedictions are recited or sung over a goblet of wine. Sometimes this is done by various guests. The bride and groom drink again from the goblet, and the groom then crushes a glass with his right foot.

The rabbi invokes the priestly blessing. The newly married couple then sign the civil contract of marriage (if they have not already had a civil wedding) and are then taken to a private room where they spend a short time together and break their fast, which commenced at dawn, before going on to the reception venue.

Hindu ceremony

Some Hindu weddings take place in halls adjoining temples, but more often than not venues such as civic suites and function rooms in hotels are used. The atmosphere at a Hindu wedding is colourful, noisy and fun, and many members of the couple's family, as well as their friends, are involved. The bride and groom sit under a canopy (*mandap*) or on a stage decorated with flowers, and a priest chants prayers and lights the sacred fire (*agni*). A Hindu wedding is valid only if the couple is married in front of a fire, said to be the eternal witness to the sacrament of marriage.

There are numerous variations to the wedding ceremony and its rituals, depending on the part of India, and even the individual community, from which the families come, and so the festivities could take up the best part of a day or even be spread over a couple of days. The single most important ritual, common to all Hindu ceremonies, is the *saptapadi*, the seven steps, or sometimes seven complete circuits, around the sacred fire taken by the bride and groom. The priest recites a series of *mantras* as the steps are taken, and asks Lord Vishnu to bless the bride and groom with food, strength, piety, children, wealth, comfort and health.

Another ritual observed at all Hindu weddings is the exchange of garlands of fragrant flowers between bride and groom as a symbol of their sharing the fragrance of life henceforth. Additionally, in most parts of India, especially the south, the tying of the *mangalsutra* is considered to be very important. A thread is knotted around the bride's neck: she will wear it (and a gold necklace, given at the same time), like a wedding ring, for the rest of her married life. (Hindu couples getting married in the West sometimes choose to have wedding rings.) A ritual that is essential in most north Indian weddings is the applying of *sindoor* (vermilion powder) to the parting of the bride's hair by the groom to indicate that she is married.

There are many other rituals, but none of these is by any means universal. *Mehendi*, the application of henna patterns to the bride's hands and feet, is a social occasion, which takes place a few days before the wedding, and is a women-only function, for family and close friends. During the wedding ceremony itself, in many parts of India the father gives the bride away (*kanya danam*), by reciting words from the epic story *Ramayana*, and pouring water on the couple's hands to symbolise the relinquishing of his parental authority. A very emotional custom, the *vidai* (departure), may take place at the end of the day-long ceremonies, as the bride's parents, close relatives and friends bid her farewell. Both bride and groom touch the feet of the elders as a mark of respect and to gain blessing for their new life.

Many families have social receptions in the evening; food, music and dancing all add to the sense of occasion.

Sikh ceremony

The Sikh culture has embraced some Hindu traditions and there are similarities between the wedding ceremonies of the two cultures. Like the Hindu ceremony, the Sikh ceremony takes place in the morning and celebrations can last the whole day. The wedding ceremony is a formal event usually held in the temple (*gudwara*). Inside the temple, guests must remove their shoes, wash their hands and cover their heads. In the prayer hall, the congregation sit on the floor facing the altar. After some prayers, the priest requests the bride's father to take one end of the brightly decorated long scarf (*laar*) which is draped round the groom's shoulders, and place it in the bride's hand. The other end is held by the groom. This signifies that the father is now giving his daughter away and that the couple are now partners who share one life. This is an emotional moment for the bride and her family. The couple hold the ends of the scarf throughout the ceremony.

The central part of the ceremony – *laama* — follows, when the groom leads the bride around the altar four times. Finally a hymn is sung to indicate that the couple are now married and the ceremony is over. Close relatives then take turns to bless the couple with garlands, sweetmeats and money. All the other guests then come up to the couple and offer gifts of money.

The departure (*dhol*) takes place at the end of the day and is a very emotional time for the bride's family and relatives. Each member wishes her good luck and bids her farewell as she leaves for her new home with the groom and his family. Today, especially in the West, the bride and groom may have already set up their own home, but it is still customary for them to spend the first few days after the wedding in the groom's family home so that the bride can get used to her new family. After that the couple may go on honeymoon.

Muslim ceremony

The wedding ceremony need not take place in a mosque, and any respected male may officiate. The bride is asked if she consents to the marriage. She may convey her consent through her guardian, usually her father, or she may answer herself. The groom is then asked if he accepts the marriage, with the agreed dowry that he will give to the bride.

These are the elements of the ceremony which are needed to meet Islamic requirements, but different cultures include extra traditions. After the wedding a celebration for the couple's families, friends and neighbours may be held days, or even weeks, later.

Wedding rehearsals

Many ministers encourage couples to have a wedding rehearsal about a week before the actual day. This is so that everyone in the wedding party knows exactly what to do and when on the day. It is attended by the bride and groom, best man, chief bridesmaid and bride's father. Other, younger attendants may be included if you wish.

Chapter 19

Organising the reception

The reception accounts for a large percentage of the cost of the wedding. The exact amount depends on how long the reception lasts, the number of guests, the venue and the type of meal and entertainment. To determine what sort of reception you would like ask yourselves:

- **how formal should the reception be**? This will affect your choice of venue, food and drink
- **how long will it last**? Shorter receptions are just as enjoyable as those that continue into the early hours of the morning and leave both you and your guests less tired. This can be an important factor if you are setting off on a long journey to your honeymoon destination that day
- **what time of day will the reception begin**? The meal served will depend on the time of day you get married. Many people marry in the mid-afternoon so that they can serve an early evening meal followed by entertainment. However, you could have a late-morning ceremony followed by a lunch and leave during the afternoon
- **how many guests will be at the reception**? Some people have a fairly brief reception immediately after the wedding for a small number of close family and friends, then throw a big party for everyone else on their return from honeymoon, while others have a quiet ceremony but invite more people to come along to all, or part, of the reception.

Juliet and Peter

Juliet and Peter had intended to fly off to the USA on the evening of their wedding day. 'In the end we had to change our plans because we couldn't get on the flight we wanted. I was very glad about this when it came to the day because although our reception, a sit-down lunch in a restaurant, ended at 5pm, I was feeling exhausted by then. Neither of us had slept well for the previous couple of nights with pre-wedding nerves, we'd both been up since 7am rushing around getting ready, and I'd hardly sat down during the reception because I was busy going round the tables talking to friends. We took a taxi from the reception to a good hotel, where we unwound over a light supper and spent the evening lazing about and talking over the day.'

Choosing a venue

Popular venues include hotels, restaurants, function rooms in pubs and sports clubs, village halls, marquees, your own or your parents' home. Allow plenty of time to shop around for a venue and compare costs carefully, as there can be huge variations between the prices of hiring the room, catering and wine. When you book a venue, confirm all the details in writing and leave nothing to chance. You can copy and complete the venue checklists given on pages 169–71, 173 and 175. The hotel checklist includes space for details of food, wine and entertainment, as these would be part of the total package. If you are using another type of venue, you will find separate checklists for food, drink and entertainment on pages 183, 186 and 199.

Before you settle on any restaurant or hotel, have a meal there so that you can judge whether the food is good, the facilities adequate and the atmosphere right.

Wherever you hold your reception, check the following:

- Is the room you would use large enough? Allow at least one square metre per person
- Are there enough toilets and sufficient cloakroom space?
- Are there plenty of parking spaces?
- Are there facilities for disabled guests or people who are elderly and frail? Some seating should be available even if the guests are to remain standing at the reception

- Is a separate room available where children could be entertained?
- How far is the reception venue from the place where the ceremony will be held? Try to keep the distance reasonably short.

Hotels

Most hotels can comfortably accommodate wedding parties of 50 to 100 guests, and some can cater for substantially more. At places where wedding receptions are held frequently, you should be able to arrange a package that includes all the catering, catering staff, wine and other drinks; the fee may also cover flowers, entertainment and a toastmaster. Check whether the venue can supply a cake stand and knife, a room where you can change into your going-away clothes, overnight accommodation for guests who need it and a safe place for displaying your wedding gifts.

The benefit of having your reception in a hotel is that you do not have to organise so much yourselves as the hotel will arrange the food, drink, entertainment and so on. Also, if you have chosen to have your civil wedding ceremony at a hotel, you will not have to travel anywhere to get to the reception. However, hotels can be an expensive option; they can be rather impersonal, especially if a large number of receptions are held there; you may have to share some facilities if another reception is taking place on the same day; hotels often need to be booked many months in advance; and there may be restrictions on the amount of time you can spend there.

Hotel checklist

Name of hotel	
Address	
Telephone/fax/email	
Contact	
Date booking made	
Confirmed in writing	
Number of guests	
Time of arrival at venue	

Time of departure from venue	
Which rooms have been booked?	
Bar facilities	
Cloakroom/toilet facilities	
Any shared facilities?	
Heating requested	
Toastmaster booked	
Who will provide flowers?	
Where will flowers be put?	
Other decorations	
Where will gifts be displayed?	
Are they insured at the hotel?	
Where will bride and groom change?	
Is a room available for children?	

Food

Type of seating plan agreed on	
Which dishes will be served?	
Any special dietary requirements?	
Number of children's portions	
How many serving staff will be available?	
What time will the meal be served?	
Cost per head of food	

Drinks

	Type of drink	Quantity	Cost per bottle
On arrival			
With the meal			
After the meal			

Evening bar				
Corkage, if supplying own drinks				
Total cost of drink				£

Entertainment

Background music provided by			
From (time)	To (time)		Breaks
Cost	£		
Dance music provided by			
From (time)	To (time)		Breaks
Cost	£		
Children's entertainment provided by			
From (time)	To (time)		Breaks
Cost	£		

Summary of costs

(a) Total cost of food	£
(b) Total cost of drink	£
(c) Total cost of entertainment	£
(d) Cost of hiring the venue	£
(e) Other items (make a detailed list)	£
(f)	£
(g)	£
(h)	£
(i)	£
(j)	£
(k) Service charge	£
Tips	£
VAT	£
TOTAL COST	£
Deposit paid	£
Balance due	£

Halls

If you have a smaller number of guests and a tight budget, consider hiring a hall or function room. Although rooms like these can be very well decorated and equipped, this is not always the case, so do pay a visit and check the facilities before making a booking. You will pay a fee for hiring the hall but will have to arrange catering and entertainment etc. yourself. Check:

- if there are any rules about the consumption of alcohol and smoking on the premises
- that the hall can be heated adequately
- whether you need to hire crockery, glasses etc.
- what facilities exist for preparing and serving food: for example, how much refrigerator and worktop space is available; whether the facilities for clearing away and washing up are good; and if you want hot food whether there are enough ovens
- whether you will need to arrange for clearing away and washing up to be done
- that the seating is comfortable and there is enough of it
- whether there is a separate room where you can change
- that the venue's insurance covers loss of or damage to gifts
- how far ahead you need to book
- that someone can show you where everything is and how it works in advance
- how long before the event you can get access for decorating the hall and for caterers to set up.

Other hired venues

These include restaurants, or rooms in stately homes, castles, river boats, and so on. The number of possible venues to choose from is enormous, especially if you want to hold your reception some-where a bit different.

Points to remember are:

- your favourite restaurant may be able to offer superb food, but you need to check that it also has facilities for changing, parking and so on. You also need to make sure that the tables can be arranged so that, ideally, everyone can see the bride and groom. There may not be space for dancing or any sort of live entertainment

- if you book a sumptuous room in a historical building you may have to hire or order many extra items, such as food and drink, tables, chairs, cutlery and crockery, glasses, serving staff, ovens and refrigerators. Even if the fee for the room itself is reasonable, these extras can add dramatically to the overall cost, so work out your budget carefully before committing yourself
- you need to check any time restrictions. Restaurants, for instance, often ask wedding parties to leave by about 5pm so that they can clear the room and lay the tables for the evening.

Venue checklist

Name of venue	
Address	
Telephone/fax	
Contact	
Date booking made	
Confirmed in writing	
Number of guests	
Time of arrival at venue	
Time of departure from venue	
When is access available before the reception?	
What are the arrangements for clearing away/locking up?	
Is smoking allowed?	
Is there a licence to serve alcohol?	
Parking facilities	
Cloakroom/toilet facilities	
Bar facilities	
Kitchen facilities	
Tables/chairs available?	
What do we need to hire separately?	

(continued overleaf)

Heating requested	
Where will flowers be put?	
Who will supply them?	
Other decorations	
Who will arrange the flowers and decorations?	
Where will gifts be displayed?	
Where will bride and groom change?	
Is a room available for children?	
What does the cost include?	
VAT	£
TOTAL COST	£
Deposit paid	£
Balance due	£

Hiring a marquee

Those who wish to hold their reception at home but who do not have enough space inside the house can hire a marquee. However, you do need a large open space to accommodate it and it can be as expensive as holding the reception at a hotel (depending on the size and quality of the marquee). Marquees are ideal in late spring, summer and early autumn but you can have one in winter as long as you have adequate heating. At any time of the year you should make plans in case of wet weather. If you choose this option you have to arrange catering, drinks, decorations etc. yourself.

Marquee checklist

Name of supplier	
Address	
Telephone/fax	
Contact	
Date booking made	
Confirmed in writing	
Size	
Number of guests	
When will the marquee be erected?	
Electricity supply	
Flowers and decorations	
When will the marquee be removed?	
Cost of marquee	£
Extras booked	
Lining	£
Coconut matting	£
Dance floor	£
Spotlights	£
Chandeliers	£
Heating	£
Tables and chairs (no.)	£
Portable toilets	£
Other	£
VAT	£
TOTAL COST	£
Deposit paid	£
Balance due	£

The caterers will work in an adjoining tent (so allow for this when working out how much space you need for the marquee) and may need access to the kitchen in the house. Choose a caterer who has worked in marquee before. You will also have to make sure that the marquee supplier provides enough electricity for the caterers to cook and run a fridge. Once you have decided on your menu, the caterers will be able to tell you what equipment they will be using; you can then pass this information to the marquee supplier, who can then arrange the correct electricity supply. The marquee is usually put up three or four days before the event.

Checkpoints for hiring a marquee:

- if you are having the marquee in your garden, warn neighbours in advance about the influx of guests, noise levels and increase in demand for parking
- make sure you have allowed sufficient space for guests to assemble for a drink before the main reception
- it is useful, particularly in cold or wet weather, to be able to walk straight out of your house into the marquee. It is ideal if you have French windows that can open directly into the marquee, but if you don't the marquee provider can construct a covered walkway from one of the doors of the house
- extras, which add to the cost of the marquee, include: lining, coconut matting, dance floor, chandelier lighting, heating, tables and chairs, portable toilets
- you will have to pay VAT but may be able to save on the overall cost by booking well in advance
- if you would like to have hanging baskets, the marquee provider can put in place ropes from which to hang them
- a 25 per cent deposit is usually requested on booking and is non-returnable.

Holding the reception in your house/flat

Home-based receptions involve a lot of work for the organisers but can have a very relaxed and informal atmosphere. The cost is relatively low, especially if you produce the food yourself. However, if you do not want to take on the job of feeding everyone, you can hire a caterer.

Checkpoints for having the reception at home:

- be realistic about the number of people you can accommodate in comfort
- check whether you have enough crockery, tables etc. If not, you may be able to borrow or hire them
- if you are going to hire caterers, make sure you have adequate facilities for them
- enlist lots of help from family and friends and delegate as much as you can
- tell neighbours well in advance about the increase in noise levels and demand for parking.

Home checklist

Number of guests	
Parking arrangements	
Which rooms will be used?	
Cloakroom/toilet facilities	
What arrangements have been made for flowers and other decorations?	
What items do we need to hire?	
Who will help?	

The food

Having decided on the venue, the next decisions you need to make are what sort of food to serve and who will prepare it. If you are using a hotel or restaurant, the food will be prepared as part of the overall package, and you will be offered a choice of menus for different types of meal, each priced per head. For other venues you will probably want to use an outside caterer.

Choosing a caterer

Book early, but not until you have compared various services and received several estimates. Personal recommendation is always preferable, otherwise you should follow up references from any caterers you are considering. Once you have chosen a caterer, you will need to supply the following information:

- the date and time of your reception
- the facilities available at the location
- the budget per head and estimated number of guests
- the kind of meal you would like
- whether any guests have special dietary requirements (although this information may not be available until you have had replies from all your guests)
- whether you would like them to supply champagne and wine (see pages 184–7).

Most caterers will supply you with a number of sample menus to choose from and should be able to add any other dishes that you particularly want. Check whether the price includes:

- tables and chairs
- table linen
- crockery, cutlery and glasses
- flowers
- serving staff
- cloakroom attendants
- clearing up after the event.

Also check whether:

- for a buffet, you are being charged per person or per plate. Some caterers charge extra for second helpings
- bread, for example, is charged as an extra
- you are expected to pay for the catering staff to have a meal during the reception
- VAT is included
- tips are expected, or a service charge is added to the fee.

Sort out all these points before you confirm the price, both verbally and then in writing. Tell the caterers of any last-minute additions or deletions to the guest list. You will be expected to pay for the number of meals ordered, even if on the day some guests do not attend.

What sort of food?

When choosing the food for your reception, remember that, particularly with large numbers of people, you are catering for a wide range of tastes. If you want to choose some adventurous options, make sure you also include some dishes that appeal across the board. It is wise to include a vegetarian option as well, and some plainer food for children.

Sit-down meal

This is the most formal, and most expensive, option. Although it provides a welcome opportunity for guests to sit down, it also limits their chances to mingle, due to the constraints of a seating plan (see pages 189–90). For a reception that continues for several hours, however, a sit-down meal provides a good opportunity for guests to relax for a couple of hours before the entertainment begins.

Buffet meal

A buffet meal can be cheaper than a sit-down meal as you need only one or two people to serve the food from the main table (unlike a sit-down meal, where you need a number of people to serve at each table). If you prefer, guests could help themselves. Buffet food can be just as substantial as a sit-down meal, but it is perhaps easier to provide a wider choice, such as a vegetarian option, a fish dish and a meat dish, with a variety of vegetables and salads. Guests can then choose exactly what they like. You could arrange a seating plan or let guests find their own seats once they have selected their food. At a large reception, it could take 30 minutes for guests to be served from a buffet.

Canapés and finger buffets

Trays of canapés and cocktail snacks can be taken round by catering staff and offered to guests. Choose foods that are easily managed with fingers if the food is to be eaten standing and serve everything in bite-sized portions, avoiding foods that crumble or drip.

For a finger buffet choose eight to ten different canapés and budget for 12 or more pieces per head. Cold foods are the easiest option, but a few hot items are always welcome. Hot canapés can be greasy, so serve them on sticks or mini forks and provide napkins. If serving them straight from trays, ensure that hot items are offered at a temperature suitable for eating immediately.

Tip

Double-check the portion sizes with caterers and err on the side of generosity. There is nothing worse than a buffet table that runs dry before everyone has been served.

Hiring a caterer checklist

Name of caterer	
Address	
Telephone/fax/email	
Contact	
Date booking made	
Confirmed in writing	
Number of guests to be served	
Number of children's portions	
What dishes are being served?	
Any special dietary requirements?	
Number of serving staff	
Does the cost include:	
Tables and chairs	

Table linen	
Crockery, cutlery and glasses	
Flowers	
Ovens	
Refrigerators	
Serving staff	
Cloakroom attendants	
Clearing up	
Are the caterers providing drinks? If so, what types and amounts are agreed?	
Corkage charge	£
How and when will caterers get access?	
Electricity supply needed	
Cost per head of food	£
Cost of drink	£
Extra costs (itemise)	
Service charge	£
Tips	£
VAT	£
TOTAL COST	£

Catering at home

Tackle this only if you are sure that you – or your friends and family – are happy to take on this extra task at an already busy time. If you feel you can cope, this is a good way to save money. Start the preparations well in advance and ask your neighbours and friends if they have any spare capacity in their freezers. Unless you are an accomplished caterer, go for simplicity.

You will also need to be able to make tea or coffee for your guests, so make sure you have the means to do this and hire anything you are lacking, for example a large urn for heating water, extra crockery or perhaps a large coffee filter machine. Remember to enlist people to help with setting up as well as clearing up, both during and after the reception. Keep a list of who is doing what, who has loaned what and what has been hired.

You will need a large table to lay out the buffet. Arrange the food in a logical order, either starting at one end and working down to the other, or starting at both ends and working towards the centre. Place plates, cutlery and napkins at the starting points.

One month or more before the wedding

- Finalise menu and start making any dishes that can be frozen.
- Make notes while you are preparing the food of anything needed for serving, such as garnishes or cream.
- Arrange to borrow or hire any equipment you need.

A week before the wedding

- Double-check that you have everything you need and confirm orders for hired items and drinks.
- Order bread for delivery/collection on the day.
- Make any dishes that can be refrigerated until needed.
- Two days before, buy perishables such as cheese, salads, fruit and cream.

The day before

- Take frozen dishes out of the freezer.
- Lay the buffet table and put out glasses, crockery and cutlery.

On the day

- Ask someone who is not going to the wedding to garnish the food and set it out on the table no more than two hours before it is to be eaten. Leave chilled dishes in refrigerator until shortly before serving.
- Prepare the salads.
- Chill wines.
- Arrange hot dishes ready for reheating.
- Dress salads just before serving.

Catering at home checklist

Number of adult guests			
Number of children			
Food			
Dishes chosen			
Any special dietary needs			

Dish	No. of portions	Who will prepare it?	Where will it be stored?	What is needed to serve it?

Other foods needed (bread, dressings etc.)

Crockery, cutlery etc.	How many are needed?	Borrow/ hire	Who from?
Setting out, serving, clearing away			
Task	When should it be done?		Who will do it?

The drink

If you have decided to hold your reception at a hotel or restaurant the drinks will almost certainly be provided as part of the overall package, and you will need to discuss which wines to serve when you make the catering arrangements.

If you are using caterers at home or at another venue they may also provide the wine, but it could be worth your while doing some cost comparisons, as you might be able to save money by providing the wine yourself. Caterers usually charge a corkage fee for handling and serving the drinks if you do this, but they may provide glasses and ice. It pays to check corkage fees carefully, as they can make a serious dent in any savings you make by buying your own wines. Although some venues and caterers do not impose a fee, the majority do charge you for the privilege of providing your own drink. The amount charged per bottle varies widely, but you're unlikely to be asked for less than £5, and quotes of £8 per bottle and upwards are not unusual.

For a hired venue such as a hall or stately home, check that it has a licence to consume alcohol; if not, you can apply for a temporary (occasional) licence from the magistrate's court.

On arrival

It is usual to serve guests with a drink as soon as they arrive at the reception or have been greeted by the receiving line. Champagne, buck's fizz, sparkling wine or a choice of medium or dry sherry are all traditional, but a glass of red or white wine – or, in winter, mulled wine – would also be acceptable. Non-alcoholic drinks should be available throughout the reception for drivers, non-drinkers and children; these could include fruit juices, mineral water, soft drinks both fizzy and still, and, if you like, non-alcoholic wines and beers.

With the meal

You can limit the choice by serving sparkling wine, or even champagne if your budget can stretch to it, throughout the proceedings. Alternatively, you can serve a choice of red or white wine throughout the meal.

For the toasts

Champagne is the traditional choice, but many excellent sparkling wines are much cheaper.

After the meal

Most guests appreciate tea or coffee at the end of the meal. If the reception is going on into the evening you can continue to serve wine and non-alcoholic drinks or let guests choose their own drinks from the bar, if there is one. You can either foot the bill throughout the evening or pay for drinks up to a pre-arranged limit, after which guests buy their own. During a reception that goes on for several hours in the evening, it is a good idea to offer tea or coffee again, mid-way through the proceedings.

Providing the drinks yourself

This is a money-saving option if you are holding the reception at a hired venue or at home. Shop around local off-licences. Most will offer champagne and wine on a sale-or-return basis. You could also consider buying from a supermarket, especially if you have time to wait for a suitable offer to appear. If you live near a Channel port and have the time, it could be worthwhile buying your wine and champagne in France. Do some research before you go, and take a detailed shopping list with you – it is easy to get carried away, and the object is to end up making a saving. However, remember that you will have to provide proof at customs that the alcohol you are bringing back to the UK is for your wedding and not for resale.

Off-licences will often deliver the wine and supply glasses free if you order all your drink from them. You may even be able to return the glasses unwashed – it is certainly worth asking, as this can be a big chore. Hire enough glasses for one-and-a-half times the number of guests. For a reception held at home, put one or two people in charge of serving the drinks. At a hired venue you could consider hiring the services of a bartender, but check his or her references before booking.

Your off-licence or local supermarket may sell ice, or you might find a supplier who can deliver ice on the day through the *Yellow Pages*. To chill white wine and champagne, float bottles in plastic rubbish bins filled with ice and water. One case of wine takes an hour to cool, and you can move chilled bottles to the top of the bins and put more in underneath as you start to use them. Still white wine can be opened ahead of time, and the corks pushed gently back in until the wine is needed.

Providing the drinks yourself checklist

	What will be served?	Quantity	Cost
On arrival			
With the meal			
For the toasts			
After the meal			
Total cost of drinks	£		
Cost of glass hire	£		
Corkage	£		
Ice	£		
Bar staff	£		
Other costs			
TOTAL COST	£		

Estimating quantities

One bottle of wine or champagne serves six glasses, or twelve if it is being mixed with orange juice for buck's fizz. During a reception lasting three hours each guest will, on average, consume half a bottle of wine. This allows for those who drink far less than this. If the reception is going on for longer you should increase this allowance accordingly. It is always better to over-estimate (if you buy on a sale-or-return basis, you can always get a refund if you have any drink left over).

Hiring a toastmaster

For a formal wedding with a large number of guests you could consider hiring a toastmaster. Hotels will be able to organise this for you, or you may find someone suitable through the *Yellow Pages* or the Guild of International Professional Toastmasters.* A toastmaster announces the guests as they arrive, makes an announcement when the meal is to be served, introduces the speech-makers, announces the cake-cutting ceremony and tells guests what the order of events will be afterwards. The best man or another male guest can be asked to perform these tasks instead if you prefer.

Reception stationery and decorations

You can personalise your reception with printed items, ranging from menus, place cards, napkins and coasters to matchbooks, napkin rings, small boxes of sweets and ribbons. You will find a wide range of designs at stationers or specialist printers, who advertise in bridal magazines. Order items about three months before the wedding day. You can save money by writing menus and place cards by hand on plain white or coloured card, or by designing them yourself on a computer (see pages 69–70). You can buy favours such as little boxes of sugared almonds from chain store bridal departments or confectioners. For information on where to use flowers at the reception, see page 114. Other decorations, such as banners or balloons, can be printed with your names and the date of the wedding if you wish. A cracker at each place is also a fun extra. An evening could end with fireworks if the venue is suitable. Look for companies who can put on a display in the *Yellow Pages*.

Chapter 20

At the reception

When planning your reception, it is vital to work out a careful timetable. Allow enough time for all the guests to arrive, be greeted and mingle whilst having a drink but do not keep them waiting too long before the meal is served (if you are having one). Allow for the meal to be served and eaten unhurriedly, then add some time for the speeches, toasts and cutting the cake. If you are leaving the reception at this point, the guests can mingle again while you get changed, and can then say their goodbyes. Otherwise, give an interval for people to move around and stretch their legs before they are seated again for any entertainment and dancing that is to follow the meal. Remember that the reception might start late if the ceremony overruns (which could be a result of the bride arriving late, the service taking longer than you thought or the photographs taking a long time). So build some contingency time into your timetable, just in case. You can delegate someone to be 'in charge' of the reception on the day and give him or her a list of contact numbers for all suppliers involved, and a detailed timetable. See page 34 for reception etiquette at second marriages.

The receiving line

At a formal wedding you can have a full receiving line to greet guests as they arrive. If you are using a toastmaster he can announce the name of each guest. The traditional order for the receiving line is:

- bride's mother
- bride's father
- groom's mother

- groom's father
- bride
- groom
- best man (if he arrives at the reception from the church in time)
- chief bridesmaid.

Time spent talking to each guest should be kept brief, otherwise guests will have to queue. To prevent delays, and to give a more informal start to the reception, the two of you could greet the guests on your own or you could circulate among them as they arrive, making sure you talk to everyone present. You could ask guests to sign a wedding book (see page 90) at this point, and this might also be an opportunity for some more photographs to be taken while your guests are chatting.

Q *My parents divorced acrimoniously years ago and refuse to speak to each other, never mind stand together in the receiving line. What shall I do?*

A For a formal receiving line, they could stand in the following order: bride's mother, groom's father, bride's father, groom's mother. However, it is probably best to dispense with a formal receiving line altogether and greet the guests without your parents, who can mingle separately.

Seating plans

If you are having a sit-down meal (or perhaps a buffet) you will need to give some thought to a seating plan. Traditionally, the newly-weds sit with their families at the top table, sitting in the following order, from left to right facing the table:

- chief bridesmaid
- groom's father
- bride's mother
- groom
- bride
- bride's father
- groom's mother
- best man.

Although this is the convention, you can alter it to suit your needs, perhaps including another family member to partner an unaccompanied parent, for instance, or changing the positions of the best man and chief bridesmaid.

Q *My parents are divorced and re-married. How do I organise the seating plan for the top table?*

A If the wedding is being hosted by your parents, you could stick with the convention and seat your parents at the top table and your step-parents at other tables close by among the other guests. If everyone gets along reasonably well there is no reason why both parents and step-parents should not be seated at the top table.

As far as the other tables are concerned, people closest to the bride and groom should sit nearest the top table. The rule is that married couples do not sit together at wedding receptions. However, rules are made to be broken and you should seat people where you think they will be happiest. It is a good idea to mix up groups of say, friends and work colleagues among relatives and other guests during the meal, especially if the reception is going on into the evening, so that guests can meet new people, and friends will have a chance to catch up with each other later on. If the meal is the only opportunity people will have to socialise, you could seat friends nearer to each other.

Be especially thoughtful when seating people who have come on their own or who know very few people at the reception and place them next to someone who can be relied on to include them in the conversation.

Tip

Do not write out the master seating plan, which will displayed on the day, too early as guests may drop out at the last minute or ask if they can bring someone extra along. If this happens you may have to swap a lot of people round to accommodate the changes and perhaps write out the seating plan a second time.

Tom and Mandy

The only hiccup on Tom and Mandy's wedding day was that the hotel laid out the tables to a completely different plan from that agreed.

'We'd been offered a choice of two table layouts to accommodate our 100 guests. We'd chosen one and then spent hours working out who was sitting next to whom. When we walked into the dining room after the wedding and all the guests had taken their places we found the tables were facing the wrong way, so we did not have the view of the sea we'd wanted from the top table, and guests who were supposed to be sitting right next to the top table were as far away as was possible. Not only did the hotel not apologise, but they said that they could not fit everyone in using the configuration we'd asked for – which was one that they had originally suggested. My advice would be to double-check that everyone can be seated as you would like before you spend any time on the detailed seating plan, and confirm the arrangements a couple of days before.'

Toasts and speeches

As guests reach the end of the meal, the toastmaster, or best man if he is acting as master of ceremonies, asks for silence so that the speeches may be made. Some couples like to cut the cake before the speeches so that it can be sliced into portions while the speeches are being made and served with coffee immediately afterwards. Otherwise, you can have the cake cutting ceremony afterwards.

The main purpose of the speeches is to thank publicly everyone who has contributed to the success of the day; to introduce the toasts to the bride and groom and bridesmaids; to entertain the guests briefly with thoughts on marriage, reminiscences about the bride and groom and so on. The best speeches are brief. None should last much more than five minutes, and three minutes would be plenty for the bride's father and groom.

If you are nervous at the prospect of making a speech, remember that the guests will be warmly disposed towards you, and the happy atmosphere on the day will help to carry you along. A sincere speech, even if it is quite brief, will be well received. That said, no one who feels that the prospect of making a speech would ruin their day should be made to do so. If this applies to you, you could decide to give the very briefest of thanks before proposing the toast or even ask someone else who enjoys public speaking to give the speech in your place. See page 34 for advice on speeches at second marriages.

The bride's father

He is the first to speak and should keep his speech fairly brief and to the point. If, for any reason, the bride's father is not present, the person who gave her away, or another close relative, can be asked to give the speech instead. In his speech the bride's father should:

- greet the guests and thank them for coming
- congratulate the groom and welcome him into the family, perhaps also mentioning the groom's parents
- end the speech by proposing a toast to the bride and groom. This can be made to 'the bride and groom', 'the happy couple' or he can use the couple's names.

During his speech, the bride's father can talk about the pleasure he has had from raising his daughter and include one or two anecdotes about her childhood or growing up. He can also offer the couple advice on marriage, speaking from his own experience, if he wishes.

The groom

The groom replies to the toast on behalf of the bride and himself. His speech may be a little longer than that of the bride's father. He should:

- thank the bride's father for the toast. He should also thank the bride's parents for allowing him to marry their daughter and, if applicable, for their generosity in hosting the wedding
- thank the guests for attending the wedding and for their gifts
- say something about his good fortune in meeting his bride and his confidence in their future happiness together. He can include one or two anecdotes about their courtship if he wishes
- mention his own parents and thank them for all they have done for him, both in bringing him up and in helping with the wedding preparations
- give special thanks to everyone who has helped with the wedding day, mentioning in particular any friends or family members who have made a special contribution, and the best man

- finally, praise the bridesmaids for their role during the day and propose the toast saying either, 'to the bridesmaids' or using their names.

The best man

The best man makes the final speech. He can speak for a little longer than the other two and can include one or two jokes or amusing anecdotes, bearing in mind his audience, which is likely to range from children to elderly relatives. However, he can also take the opportunity to say something more serious about his relationship with the groom and what it means to him. He should:

- thank the groom for the toast on behalf of the bridesmaids
- congratulate the newly-wed couple
- thank anyone connected with the wedding who has given him particular help
- end his speech with a toast to the bride and groom
- finally, read out any telemessages, emails or cards that have been received, first vetting them for unsuitable comments. If there are a great many he could read one or two messages and list the names of other senders

Q *Can the bride make a speech? I don't like the idea of sitting in silence and would love the opportunity to say thank you as well for all the help we have had in the run up to the wedding.*

A There is no reason why you shouldn't make a speech, and an increasing number of brides choose to do so. You can speak before the groom and ask your father to give you an introduction, or after the groom, before the toast to the bridesmaids, which means the groom will have to stand again to make the toast. Otherwise you could make your speech a little later in the proceedings, after the cake has been cut and before guests rise and move into a different room. Your speech can be similar in tone to the groom's, thanking your family and the guests, and saying something affectionate about your new husband.

How to write and deliver a good speech

- The key to giving a good speech is to **plan it in advance**.
- **Don't write the speech out and read it word for word**, as this will make your delivery stilted. Instead, write key points with a few memory-jogging phrases for each on a series of numbered cards, which can be kept in your pocket until they are needed. Practise the speech beforehand so that it becomes very familiar, then use the cards as prompts to guide you through the speech. This method also allows you to improvise or add to the speech if something occurs to you on the day and will help to make the speech sound more spontaneous.
- **Organise your speech so that it gets off to a lively start and engages the audience's attention.** The middle section should be the longest, and you should conclude with a neat lead in to the toast at the end.
- **Make a special note of all the people you have to thank**, with links or brief anecdotes next to them.
- **Read out the draft of your speech and time it**. Then leave the draft for a day or two before looking at it again.
- **Keep the speech short and to the point** without being brusque. Don't tell long-winded jokes or anecdotes. Brief stories, which arrive quickly at their point, are the best.
- **Be careful about jokes**, especially if you are making them at someone else's expense. It is acceptable for the best man to raise a laugh at the groom's expense if it is done affectionately, but you should steer clear of humorous references to the bride's mother or the bride. Jokes should be kept clean and mild. One-liners are often more effective than longer jokes.
- You can learn a lot about how to improve your delivery simply by **taping the speech and listening to it carefully**. You can also try it out on trusted friends and judge the effect of any jokes or anecdotes you plan to use.
- On the day, **do not have more than a couple of drinks before making your speech**. When the moment comes, try to relax, take a few steadying breaths before you rise, and smile at your audience as you begin to speak.

- **Stand naturally, with your hands at your sides, or in front of you holding your prompt cards**. Do not grasp your lapels or lean forward with your hands resting on the table.
- When delivering the speech **aim to sound neither pompous nor overly informal**. Even at a very relaxed reception a certain level of formality is appropriate for the speeches. Use everyday language rather than formal expressions but avoid slang and clichés.
- **Use your normal voice, not an assumed accent or 'stage' voice**. Keep your head up and speak clearly and not too fast.
- **Remember to breathe normally, and pause slightly between sentences to breathe**. People often 'forget' to breathe when they are nervous, and you can find yourself running out of breath towards the end of a sentence.
- **Keep your gaze just above the heads of your audience** and do not stare round at doors, windows or the ceiling. When mentioning anyone specifically or proposing a toast you should look towards the person concerned without staring or making them feel uncomfortable.
- You could look at one of the several **books of wedding speeches** – available from bookshops and libraries – for inspiration, although it is not a good idea to copy a speech verbatim. If you prefer to write a speech from scratch, books of suitable quotations, anecdotes and jokes both for weddings and for after-dinner speeches can provide material that you can weave in among stories of your own. You may also find useful material on the Internet (see page 69).

Cutting the cake

Once the speeches and toasts are over, the best man, or toastmaster, announces the cutting of the cake. The bride holds the cake knife and the groom puts his hands over hers to make the first cut. It is helpful if the cut has been discreetly started beforehand, so that you do not have to struggle to get the knife through hard icing. Photographs are usually taken at this point. One cut is all that is needed, then the cake is taken away and cut into small portions which are distributed by the bridesmaids and pages or by the waiters and waitresses.

Entertainment

You can arrange background music – either live or recorded – while the guests are arriving and eating. At a longer reception, you will also need music for dancing in the evening. Remember that it will take about 45 minutes for a band or disco to set up.

Ask for recommendations and look at advertisements in wedding magazines and the *Yellow Pages*. Try to attend a performance, or at least listen to a tape, by any musicians you are considering hiring before booking them and discuss the sort of music you have in mind to make sure it is within their range. The cost will depend on:

- how many players are involved
- how busy they are
- how long you want them to play for
- how far they have to travel
- whether you ask them to learn any new items specially for the occasion.

Confirm in writing details of the date, venue, amount payable, cancellation policy, length of time for playing and for breaks.

Orchestras, bands and groups

Hiring an orchestra or band is ideal if you have a large number of guests and want dancing to live music. Most musicians who play regularly at weddings have a suitable repertoire, which should be varied in order to appeal to the wide age range at the wedding. A barn dance or ceilidh are other options, for which you can use recorded or live music, but you would need to hire a caller to direct the dances.

You should find out what the musicians' policy on taking breaks is. Do they provide recorded music to be played while they are having their breaks or do they let one person at a time rest while the others continue playing? You will probably want some form of music to fill in the gaps if the musicians do have their breaks at the same time so it is best to know in advance if you have to make your own arrangements for this.

Ensembles and soloists

These are good for background music at a smaller venue or in addition to dance music at a large reception. You could choose a pianist, flautist, harpist, string ensemble, jazz musicians, steel band, fiddlers, medieval minstrels or singers.

Recorded music, discos and DJs

Live entertainment is not cheap, and you can keep costs down by using recorded background music. A hotel may have a selection of suitable CDs which can be played over a sound system, or at other venues you can put together your own recorded music and ask a friend to play it over your own sound system or one which has been hired or borrowed. You can provide dance music in the same way.

Using a DJ who provides a sound system and selection of music is another good way to entertain your guests and is cheaper than using live musicians. Make sure the DJ knows the types of music you want and understands that the volume must not be too loud.

Dancing

Traditionally, the bride and groom dance alone together for a few minutes before other guests join in. During the evening the bride should dance with all the men in the family party, and the groom with the women. The best man should also dance with the women of the wedding party, including the bride. In the intervals between dances the couple should circulate together and separately and make sure they speak to everyone present, taking the opportunity to thank any who have been particularly helpful towards making the day a success.

Suitable music for the first dance

- 'Hawaiian Wedding Song' sung by Andy Williams
- 'When a Man Loves a Woman' sung by Percy Sledge

- 'The First Time Ever I Saw Your Face' sung by Roberta Flack
- 'My Love' sung by Paul McCartney
- 'We've Only Just Begun' sung by The Carpenters
- 'Wonderful World' sung by Louis Armstrong
- 'My Heart Will Go On' sung by Celine Dion.

Entertainment for children

If you are having a large number of children at your wedding reception, remember that they might get bored so it could be worthwhile arranging entertainment specifically for them. If your budget allows, you could hire a professional entertainer, who could also look after them during the ceremony if you like (look in the *Yellow Pages*). Otherwise, you could arrange for a few helpers to keep an eye on the children while they are playing in a separate room. The parents of the children might be able to help on a rota basis, so that no one misses too much of the reception.

Entertainment possibilities include:

- **a professional children's entertainer** – perhaps a clown, magician, Punch and Judy or other puppet show. Some entertainers offer party packages which are intended for children's birthday parties but could be adapted for a wedding
- **a bouncy castle**
- **a children's disco**
- **a selection of videos** for the children to watch. Feature-length cartoons are popular
- some companies, such as the Wedding Crèche Service★, offer an **'activity crèche'** service, where children are looked after for you and kept occupied with toys, games, storytelling, music, face painting, playdough and crayons or even gym equipment.

Entertainment checklist

Name of musicians for background music	
Address	
Telephone/fax/email	
Contact	
Date booked	
Confirmed in writing	
Arrival time	
Play from:	To:
Breaks agreed	
Where will the musicians perform?	
Particular items requested to be played	
COST	£
Deposit paid	£
Balance due	£
Name of musicians/DJ for dance music	
Address	
Telephone/fax	
Contact	
Date booked	
Confirmed in writing	
Arrival time	
Play from:	To:
Breaks agreed	
Where will the musicians perform?	

(continued overleaf)

Particular items requested to be played	
COST	£
Deposit paid	£
Balance due	£
Name of children's entertainer	
Address	
Telephone/fax	
Contact	
Date booked	
Confirmed in writing	
Entertainment agreed	
Arrival time	
Entertain from:	To:
Breaks agreed	
Where will the entertainment take place?	
VAT	
COST	£
Deposit paid	£
Balance due	£

Leaving the reception

Towards the end of the festivities the best man should tell you when it is time to change. The chief bridesmaid can help the bride, and she or the bride's mother can take charge of the bride's dress. The best man takes care of the groom's clothes, returning any hired clothes by the agreed date.

The best man makes sure your transport is ready and announces that you are ready to leave. The guests gather at the door and may throw confetti or flower petals. The bride tosses her bouquet, or a posy of flowers removed from it, into the crowd, and everyone follows the couple outside to give them a final send-off as they drive or are driven away. The couple's departure is the signal for the guests to begin leaving, and indeed no one should have left before this (although this does not apply if the party goes on until the early hours of the morning and the couple plan to stay until the end. If this is the case, it would be a good idea for the best man to announce this during the speeches).

Now is the time to settle the bill and check that nothing has been left behind by guests. The bride's parents, best man or chief bridesmaid remove the remains of the cake, the couple's wedding clothes, telemessages and cards and any flowers which they would like to take home. They also arrange for the wedding gifts to be taken somewhere for safe keeping until the couple return from honeymoon. The hosts and best man are the last to leave the reception.

Chapter 21

Insurance

When you are planning your big day, insurance will probably not be at the top of your list of things to organise, but it is worth setting some time aside to check that you will not lose out financially if anything goes wrong.

Whether or not you choose to buy one of the specialist wedding policies depends on how much money you will be investing in your wedding and the kind of mishap you are worried about. You should also bear in mind that while wedding insurance covers you up to – and including – the day itself, it does not cover you afterwards. So since you may be making large purchases (such as engagement and wedding rings) several months before the wedding and you will have your rings and wedding presents for a long time afterwards, you should check that your existing house contents insurance covers you for these things.

Do you need wedding insurance?

The main reason for buying wedding insurance is to cover yourself against the cost of having to cancel or reschedule your wedding. So whether this sort of insurance is worthwhile depends to a large extent on the cancellation fees your suppliers will charge you and whether they will waive the fees if you subsequently reschedule the wedding.

A wedding insurance policy will not cover you if you have to cancel simply because either of you has had a change of heart, or reimburse you if you knew you were going to cancel before you took out the insurance. However, in the main you will find that you can buy cover against unforeseen disasters that cause you to cancel:

- the death, illness or injury of the bride, groom or a relative – but check the definition of 'relative' carefully because it varies from policy to policy
- the inability of one of the above to attend the wedding because of jury service, redundancy, cancelled leave (if in the Armed Forces) or, with some policies, extreme weather conditions (such as being snowed in and unable to get to the wedding as a result)
- failure of suppliers (e.g. florists, caterers, wedding cars, photographers and so on) because they have gone out of business – but note that you will not be covered if a supplier simply fails to meet the terms of your contract and is still in business. This is because you can sue instead (see 'When things go wrong' on page 208)
- the ceremony or reception venue no longer being available for you to use
- being unable to find replacements for lost or damaged wedding dress, hired suits and bridesmaids' dresses.

Tip

The best insurance against failure of suppliers to deliver, is to choose reputable firms, to ensure that you have a clear written agreement and – if possible – to avoid making full and final payment until after the delivery of goods and services.

You will also find that most policies will pay out:

- for the cost of arranging alternative transport because the wedding car did not turn up
- if you managed to avoid cancelling the wedding by getting a different supplier to do the job – the most you can claim is typically 25 per cent of the original supplier's invoice
- for loss of deposits you have paid to suppliers who fail to deliver goods or services (because they have gone out of business)
- for the loss of deposits paid for live entertainment if the entertainment does not arrive (for whatever reason)
- for replacing or repairing the wedding rings (but not the engagement ring), wedding clothes (of key people) and wedding presents

if they are lost, stolen or damaged (although you may already have this cover – see 'Cover outside the home' on page 206)

- if you need to re-stage the wedding to take photographs or record a video because the original film or negatives were lost or damaged (however, no policy will pay out to re-stage the photography just because you were disappointed with the results)
- for the legal expenses involved in defending your case if you are sued by a supplier for damage you or one of your guests caused or – less probably – if a guest sues you. (However, if you are holding your reception at home, your legal liability if people injure themselves when visiting you is already covered by your contents insurance – see page 206)
- if you hire a marquee and your supplier tells you that you are responsible for insuring against damage to it. Note that this cover may be offered as an add-on for which you will have to pay more.

Tip

If you know you would not want to re-stage your wedding just for the photographs but would be disappointed if you had no record of your big day, consider appointing a friend who is good at photography to step into the breach if the need arises. Alternatively, ask your wedding guests for copies of photos they may have taken.

Buying wedding insurance

The most important consideration when buying this kind of insurance is to make sure you buy sufficient cover. After all, there is little point buying a policy which will pay out a maximum of only £3,000 if the cost of cancelling your wedding would actually be, say, £8,000. You should also check that other limits in the policy – e.g. what will be paid for re-staging photographs or damage to wedding attire – are sufficient to cover your particular wedding arrangements.

If you are offered wedding insurance by one of your suppliers, do not take it until you have compared both the cover and price with policies offered elsewhere. Policies do vary – some automatically include cover for damage to marquees, for example, while others charge extra for this kind of cover.

The price of this kind of insurance varies too. For example, to cover cancellation costs of £6,000, you could pay as little as £50 or as much as £125 – while insuring against costs of £10,000 could set you back from £100 to as much as £300.

Why you should check your existing insurance

There are two main reasons for looking at your existing insurance:

- to see whether you really need to buy special wedding insurance (see pages 202–4)
- to make sure that you have sufficient insurance for those things that a special wedding policy will not cover.

Cover for valuables

It is unlikely that you will find wedding insurance that will cover your engagement ring, and you will also find that the wedding rings are covered only if they are lost or damaged in the week leading up to the wedding. So as soon as the engagement and/or wedding rings have been bought, you should make sure that your existing contents insurance provides enough cover in case they are lost, damaged or stolen. Many contents policies have what are called 'single item' limits for valuable belongings – £1,000, for example – although it might be lower or higher. The limit represents the most that will be paid out in the event of a claim, even if the cost of replacing each ring is more than your insurer's single-item limit. You should also check the limit if your wedding dress is particularly costly.

Tip

Make sure that your fiancé(e) keeps the receipt for each ring since it may be needed as evidence if you do ever have to claim for its loss. If the ring is an antique (and so could not be replaced as new), get it professionally valued: the Incorporated Society of Valuers and Auctioneers* can provide you with a list of valuers who will undertake insurance valuations. Whether your ring is antique or new, it is a good idea to take a photograph of it (this will help to identify it if it is ever stolen).

Cover outside the home

Because you will be wearing your ring(s) when you are away from home, it is worth finding out whether you have 'all risks' cover (sometimes called 'cover away from the home'). If you do not already have this cover, expect to pay more for your insurance and note that there may be a different single-item limit so check that too. The advantage of buying an all-risks extension to your contents policy is that your belongings are usually covered when you are abroad, and some insurers will give you a discount on your travel insurance, which could be useful for the honeymoon.

It is also worthwhile checking your insurer's single-item limits and all-risks cover if you are expecting to receive particularly valuable engagement and wedding presents. This is especially important if you plan to put them on display at the reception: if you do not have all-risks cover, you may not be able to claim if something happens to them on the way to the reception venue – although this is less of a problem if your reception is held at home.

Tip

If you are getting married abroad, it is unlikely that standard travel insurance will provide the level of cover you will need to replace your rings, the wedding dress (and other wedding clothes) and any wedding presents that may be sent to you which fail to arrive at your destination or get stolen. So in addition to travel insurance, you should make sure you arrange an all-risks extension to your contents policy (which will provide better cover for your belongings than travel insurance).

Checking your contents policy

You may also need to increase the total amount you have your contents insured for (to include your rings and presents). Some house contents policies automatically provide extra cover for weddings, but for a limited amount of time only – 30 days each side of the wedding day, for example, but check your policy to make sure. With other policies, you will need to increase your cover and possibly pay a higher premium. If you are getting married in your parents' home town and a large number of presents are being brought to your wedding, it is likely that you will need your parents to look after these presents until you get back from your honeymoon. If this is the case, you will need to check your parents' house contents policy as well as your own.

Tip

If your reception is to be held at home – and especially if you are hiring outside suppliers – it is worth informing your existing insurers that this will be the case. If anything is damaged or goes missing during the reception, your insurers could refuse to pay any claims you make on the grounds that you did not tell them that there were going to be a large number of people in the house.

Insurance for the honeymoon

If you are planning to go abroad for your honeymoon, you will need to organise travel insurance. The main reason for buying travel insurance is to cover yourself against the costs of emergency medical treatment while you are abroad and the potentially very expensive bill if you are legally required to pay damages to someone whose property you have damaged or whom you have injured while on your travels. You also need additional cover for cancellation, delayed or missed departure, legal expenses and personal accident. However, if you already have an all-risks extension to your house contents policy, you may not need a travel policy to cover your money and belongings and you may be able to get a discount on your travel insurance.

You also need to check that your policy covers you for taking part in any dangerous activities – scuba diving or white-water rafting, for example. However, what you consider dangerous and what your insurer considers dangerous may differ so to be on the safe side, ask whether your planned activity is covered. If it is not or if it is specifically excluded from the cover, find another insurer.

When things go wrong

If you buy wedding insurance, you have a measure of cover if your suppliers fail to deliver but only if it is because they have gone out of business. If they simply failed to deliver what you had ordered (and they are still in business) or failed to comply fully with the terms of your contract with them, insurance will not cover you because you can seek compensation directly from the supplier. The same is true if a wedding present you are given turns out to be faulty in some way.

The Sale of Goods Act 1979 (as amended) states that goods bought from a business must comply with their 'description' and 'be of satisfactory quality' so if you ask your florist to supply red roses, for example, you should not receive pink carnations; similarly, a spin dryer you are given as a wedding present should spin. The Supply of Goods and Services Act 1982 (common law in Scotland) states that 'services' supplied by a business should be carried out with 'reasonable care and skill'. For example: hired cars should not break down, marquees should not collapse and the photographs should not be blurred. If you book your honeymoon through a tour operator, you have added protection against a substandard holiday or against the tour operator going bust in the form of the Package Travel Regulations 1992.

If you feel that your suppliers have let you down and it is not possible to get the problem sorted out before the wedding, you can ask your supplier not only to refund your money but also to compensate you for any additional expenditure you may have incurred as a result of their incompetence. You may also be able to claim for the loss of enjoyment you suffered. Where contractors know that they are providing services for a wedding, the loss-of-enjoyment factor will be greater than usual because of the one-off nature of the event. If you have a complaint, you should make your dissatisfaction known clearly and politely to the person in charge and you should follow this up in writing, explaining what you want them to do to rectify the situation and the amount of financial compensation which you expect to receive. If your supplier ignores your complaint or fails to offer you satisfactory compensation, you can pursue the matter in the small claims court (sheriff court in Scotland).

Chapter 22

Financing your future

In purely financial terms, wedded bliss is well worthwhile: as a married couple you may be able to pay less tax, your future pension will go up and, from the moment you sign your marriage certificate, you will automatically be entitled to at least some – if not all – of your spouse's wealth. How far your other finances are affected by marriage depends on more personal factors such as whether one or both of you decides to change your name, how joint you want your finances to be, how financially dependent one of you will be on the other and how keen you are to exploit the tax rules which favour the married state.

Some couples choose to draw up a prenuptial agreement, which covers how their assets would be divided in the event of a divorce. Although no one wants to consider divorce before they have even got married, some couples feel happier if they know where they stand financially. For more information on this, see pages 17–18.

Marriage and tax

Before April 1990, marriage meant that a man became responsible for his wife's tax affairs, and a woman's income from savings and investments was regarded as belonging to her husband, so he had to pay the tax on it. Since then, however, husband and wife are treated as individuals, with each responsible for their own tax affairs. This means that you will still get your own slice of tax-free income (your personal allowance), pay your own tax bill and, if applicable, have to fill in your own tax return. Apart from having to tell your tax office if you change your name, in practical terms you will see very little difference in your dealings with the Inland Revenue. Although married couples no longer get an extra personal allowance for having tied the knot, the tax system still looks favourably on married couples because:

- any **gifts** you make to each other will be free of tax
- you may be able to save tax by **rearranging the ownership of your savings and investments**.

Tax-free gifts

It may seem an odd concept that gifts attract tax at all but they do: in the form of inheritance tax for the recipient and capital gains tax for the person making certain sorts of gift (in general, things which can rise and fall in value such as antiques, property and shares). The tax rules for gifts largely exist to deter people from giving away their wealth before they die as a way of avoiding inheritance tax. So it is unlikely that you will have to tell your tax office about all your wedding presents – although it may be interested if they are very valuable. As soon as you are married, there is no need to worry about tax on anything you give to your spouse because gifts between husband and wife – whatever the gift is and whatever it is worth – are exempt from both inheritance tax and capital gains tax, which can work to your advantage (see below). The tax rules are also quite generous when it comes to wedding presents:

- before the wedding, the bride and groom can give each other gifts of up to £2,500
- each parent of the bride or groom can give one or other of them a gift up to the value of £5,000
- a grandparent (or great-grandparent) can give up to £2,500
- anyone else can give £1,000.

Note that if a gift exceeds the limits given above and the person making the gift dies within seven years of making it, there may be inheritance tax to pay if the donor's estate is worth more than a certain amount (£242,000 for deaths occurring in the 2001–2 tax year). If the gifts fall within the limits given above, there will be no inheritance tax to pay.

Tip

Strictly speaking, to qualify for their tax-free status, wedding gifts have to be made 'in consideration of the marriage' and 'conditionally on the marriage taking place', so encourage generous relatives to write you a letter which makes the reason for their gift clear.

Your savings and investments

Because husbands and wives are taxed independently of each other, you will see no change in the way your savings and investments are taxed. However, you may want to rearrange your joint finances to make the most of the tax concessions available to married couples.

- If you have **savings or investments in joint names** – a joint building society account, for example – the income is automatically treated as being paid to you in equal shares, with each of you being responsible for paying the tax on your own share. However, if you own the savings or investments in unequal shares, you can ask your tax office to tax the income on that basis – so if you paid in a third of the money held in a joint savings account and your spouse paid in two thirds, you can ask to be taxed only on one third of the income.
- Perhaps more worthwhile – **if you and your spouse pay different rates of tax or one of you pays no tax at all** – is to put the savings and/or investments solely into the name of the spouse paying less or no tax. However, you have to be prepared to relinquish control over the money you give to your spouse so think carefully if you are not happy to do this.
- If you make a lot of **capital gains** – you dabble in the Stock Market, for example – and you regularly make full use of your own capital gains tax exemption of £7,500 (in the 2001–2 tax year) consider giving your spouse any investment that you would want to sell to make use of the fact that you each get your own £7,500 exemption. However, this will not help if your spouse also makes substantial capital gains and/or refuses to sell.

Marriage and your pension

Although it is probably not at the forefront of your mind as you plan for your big day, your pension may receive a substantial boost as soon as you have tied the knot – particularly if you are a woman. If you belong to an employer's pension scheme, you are very likely to find that – without your having to increase your pension contributions – your spouse will automatically become entitled to receive a widow's or widower's pension and possibly a lump sum when you die. Depending on your spouse's National Insurance record, you may also qualify for a lump sum and allowance from the state.

If you have a personal pension, where your contributions build up a fund, this should be paid as a lump sum to your spouse in the event of your death. You can also arrange for your spouse to receive a pension if you die after retirement by buying what is called a 'joint life annuity'. The exception to this is where you have invested part of your National Insurance Contributions in a personal pension (these sorts of plans are variously called 'appropriate', 'rebate-only' or 'contracted-out' pension plans). These pension plans must make provision for a pension to be paid to your widow or widower (if 45 or over at the time of your death unless you have children).

Whichever sort of pension you have, make sure that the provider of it knows that you have married. You should tell the Contributions Agency★ (the government agency in charge of National Insurance Contributions) that you are now married as a matter of course.

Marriage, money and property: wills (England and Wales)

There is more to the toast 'health, wealth and happiness' than you may have imagined because (unless you live in Scotland, see page 214) as soon as you marry, your spouse automatically becomes entitled to at least £125,000 of all your worldly goods. This is because your marriage automatically declares any will you may have made as a single person null and void (in legal parlance, your marriage 'revokes' the earlier will). If you want to be confident that in the event of your death your spouse will get all your worldly goods, you will have to make another will in his or her favour. If you do not do this, the law decides how much he or she will get and shares out your estate – everything you own after subtracting debts and any jointly owned assets, such as your home – as follows (note that the amount of the limits given below may change from time to time):

- if your estate is worth less than £200,000 (less than £125,000 if you have children) your spouse gets everything
- if your estate is worth more than £200,000, your spouse gets £200,000 plus half the remaining estate. The rest passes to whichever generation of relatives is still alive in this order: your parents, your siblings, your nephews and nieces. If there are no relatives to inherit the remainder of the estate, your spouse gets everything
- if your estate is worth more than £200,000 and you have children, your spouse gets £125,000 plus the right to the use of and/or income from (called a life interest) half the remaining estate. Your children get the rest.

As well as making sure that your wealth goes to those people you want to have it, making a will simplifies and shortens the process of sorting out your affairs. Making a new will after your marriage is particularly important if you have children from an earlier liaison and you want them to inherit part of your estate.

Making a new will is less urgent if your matrimonial home is your main asset and it is already in your joint names since half of it, if you are 'tenants in common', will pass to your spouse through the intestacy provisions; if you are 'joint tenants', the share will pass automatically to your spouse whether or not you make a will, i.e. by survivorship.

Tip

If you want to avoid the problem of being without a will from your wedding day until you have time to make a new one after your marriage, consult your legal adviser before your wedding. Your adviser should be able to draw up a specially worded will that will not be automatically revoked by your marriage. This should say that the will is made in contemplation of marriage to a named person and it should also specifically state that the person whose will it is (the testator) intends that the will shall not be revoked by his or her marriage to the named person.

Wills in Scotland

If your permanent home is in Scotland and you die without making a will, the rules are different from those in England, Wales and Northern Ireland. Your spouse gets the house or flat (up to £110,000 in value), furniture (up to a value of £20,000) and a cash sum of £50,000 provided that there are no children or other descendants. If there are, the cash sum is reduced to £30,000. Your spouse is also entitled to half (a third if there are children) the remaining 'movable' estate – which means anything that is not land or buildings. If there is anything left after that, the remainder goes to the nearest relatives of the person who died following this order: children, grandchildren, great-grandchildren then siblings and finally parents.

Tip

To find out more about tax and marriage, ask your tax office for leaflet IR80 *Income tax and married couples.*

Marriage and your joint finances

Although you have little say in the way marriage affects your tax, pension or right to inherit, it is entirely up to you whether or not marriage has an effect on your day-to-day finances. However, it is worth spending time talking about how you will organise your finances, not least because it could spare you a few rows: according to a survey conducted early in 1998 for Relate★ (the relationship-counselling charity), money came top of the list of the reasons for marital strife, with nearly half the people in the survey saying that it was the most common cause of arguments.

If you were living together before you married, you will probably have come to some arrangement for sharing the household bills and other joint spending. However, if you are setting up home together for the first time, it would be worthwhile deciding:

- what you both agree is joint spending
- what you are each going to contribute to joint spending

- what you both agree is personal (and private) spending
- who is going to pay for what
- how you are going to share bills
- how you are going to share your assets – your home or shares, for example
- who is going to be in charge of the finances
- how you will agree spending priorities
- how you will make financial plans for the future – whether it is saving for a holiday or for when you have children.

Once you have decided all that, you will be in a position to see if you need to make any adjustments to your existing financial arrangements, such as making your bank account a joint one or arranging for your spouse to be the joint owner of your home.

Warning

According to Relate*, lack of openness in financial arrangements can be a major source of friction and can even point to an underlying lack of trust in other areas of your relationship. In the Relate survey, women were found to be particularly sensitive to trust and secrecy issues related to money.

Joint and separate bank accounts

If you decide that you are going to pool your resources (whether in whole or in part) to pay for what you have decided is joint spending, you may find it useful to open a joint bank account. You can either run this alongside your own personal current accounts – because you want to keep some of your finances separate and private, for example – or you can arrange for both your salaries (if applicable) to be paid into a joint account and close your sole accounts. An alternative, if you want to share everything with your spouse but you do not want to close your sole account – because it is convenient for work, for example – is to make both your sole accounts joint ones.

You will have to open the joint account together, but whether you both have to sign cheques is up to you. Once the account is open, you will each get your own cheque book, cheque guarantee card (provided the bank is happy to provide this straight away), payment and cash card (or 'multi-function' card which combines all three types of card). You will also become joint owners of the money in the account and jointly responsible for any debts (called 'joint and several liability'). This means that your current account provider can recover money to pay off debts from either account holder regardless of who actually spent the money.

The same is true if you arrange for your spouse to be an additional cardholder on your credit card. However, if you each have an existing credit card in your pre-marriage names, there is no particularly good reason for changing the arrangement – especially since having two different cards gives you more flexibility and possibly a higher joint credit limit. The only situation in which it could be worth making your spouse an extra cardholder on your credit card is if he or she has been refused a credit card of his or her own.

Warning

If you have a very different attitude towards money from that of your partner – one of you is a saver while the other is a spendthrift, for example – you may find it less stressful to keep your financial arrangements separate.

Medical insurance

If you have private medical insurance (which aims to pay for private health care) either through your job or that you have bought yourself, make sure that your employer or the insurer knows that you have married. If you want your spouse to benefit from the policy, you may find that it does not cost that much more to cover him or her under a joint policy.

Life insurance

If you want your spouse to benefit from any life insurance you have, you will need to tell your employers (if they provide death-in-service benefits) and also your insurers that you have married. It would also be a good idea to check that the policies are 'written in trust' to your spouse so that the proceeds will be paid directly to him or her. This has two advantages: the money can be paid more quickly, and it does not count towards your estate for inheritance tax purposes.

Appendix: Wedding law

Anyone getting married in the UK must meet the legal requirements, whether they are having a civil wedding or a religious wedding of any denomination.

The law in England and Wales

The basic rules that apply to all marriages in England and Wales are:

- the couple must be of different sexes
- you must be aged 16 or over but you need your parents' written consent if you are under the age of 18
- you must be free to marry, i.e. you must not be related to each other in any of the ways specified on pages 227–8. Also if either party has been married previously, the former marriage must have been ended by decree in the appropriate court.
- you must have two witnesses
- the wedding must take place in a district register office, in any premises approved by the local authority for marriages (hotel, stately home etc.), in a church or chapel of the Church of England or Church in Wales, in a military chapel, a synagogue or in any other place of worship that has been registered by the Registrar General for England and Wales★ for the solemnisation of marriages.

The service may not be conducted privately – which means that the doors may not be locked during the ceremony, thereby preventing potential bona fide objectors being present. The marriage (both civil and religious) may take place on any day at any time between 8am and 6pm and need only be in front of two witnesses, who can be total strangers to each other and to you. (These restrictions do not apply to Jewish or Quaker weddings.)

The law in Scotland

Marriage law in Scotland differs in a few crucial ways. The minimum legal age is 16 whether you have parental consent or not.

There are no restrictions on the time or place at which a religious marriage can take place as long as the legal and civil requirements are met. In theory, you are free to marry outdoors at midnight if you can find an authorised minister to conduct the ceremony. If you want to get married on a boat it must be tethered, and if you are marrying in a hot-air balloon it must be anchored to the ground. However, civil weddings in Scotland must take place in a register office by arrangement with the registrar.

Documents required for marriage

For a civil wedding in the UK, when making a marriage application to the registrar you should take your birth certificate or passport. For a church wedding you will need to show your certificate of baptism to the minister (and confirmation certificate, in the case of the Roman Catholic Church). Most churches require at least one of you to be baptised. If you are marrying for the second time you will need to show your decree absolute or the death certificate of your former spouse. If you are under the age of 18 consent from your parents or guardians will normally be required.

Setting the date

In the case of both civil and religious weddings in England or Wales, the date of the marriage can be set up to a year in advance, and you may be able to make a provisional booking further ahead than this. In Scotland, the amount of advance notice needed is left to the discretion of the minister or registrar, provided it meets with Scottish legal requirements (see page 223), but couples are advised to make enquiries of the minister or registrar well in advance, particularly if they live in a town or city.

Church of England weddings

If you are getting married in an Anglican church the form of service must be agreed with the minister. There are three permitted options: the traditional *Book of Common Prayer* service, the slightly revised (1966) form of that service or *The 2000 Marriage Service* (Common Worship).

The tradition of reading marriage banns, and the requirement that people must live in the parish in which they marry, are currently under review by the General Synod. At the time of writing (late 2001), the law remains as below.

Marriage by banns

You should agree the date of your wedding with the minister at the earliest opportunity. If either (or both) of you lives in the parish where you are to marry, the minister will arrange to have banns read in the church on three Sundays prior to the wedding. This is usually on consecutive Sundays and must be carried out within three months of the date of the wedding. It is customary for the couple to attend the service on those three Sundays to hear their banns read. The purpose of the banns is to make public your intention to marry and to invite any objections to the ceremony taking place. The fee for the calling of banns is £15. If one of you lives in another parish the banns must also be read in that church for which the same fee is charged, and in addition a banns certificate must be obtained from the minister of the second church, for which the fee is £9. In addition, you may choose to be married in the church where one (or both) of you worships and is on the church electoral role. In that event the banns must be called in that church and also in the parish or parishes where you both live. Banns are not called if the marriage takes place by common or special licence, as described below.

Marriage by common licence

This is used when the parties to the marriage are resident in a particular parish only temporarily, which must be a minimum of

15 consecutive days before the licence is issued. It is also used where one party to the marriage, who normally lives in England, does not have British nationality, or where one party is a British national who normally lives abroad.

As with banns, one of you must be living in the parish where you are to marry, or be on the church electoral role, and the minister will be able to advise about applying for the licence. Where a licence has been obtained no banns are called, but an affidavit – verifying the details given and that there is nothing in law to prevent the marriage – has to be sworn. The affidavit must be sworn within the three-month period before the date of the wedding. You should note that common licences are not available if one of you has been divorced (and the former spouse is still living) and it is also a requirement that at least one of you must be baptised. The fee for a common licence is currently £55.

Marriage by special licence

This licence is issued on the authority of the Archbishop of Canterbury, and exceptional reasons why one of the other preliminaries on page 220 cannot be used must be given. It is generally used where neither of you is resident in the parish where you wish to marry or if the wedding is to take place in an unlicensed building, such as a private chapel. These licences are issued by the Faculty Office,* which you should approach after consultation with the minister. Again, special licences are not available where one party is divorced, with a former spouse still living, or where neither party is baptised. The fee is currently £125.

Civil weddings in England and Wales

The former procedures for giving notice for a civil marriage by superintendent registrar's certificate either with or without licence have been replaced by a common 15-day notice procedure. These changes to the Marriage Act 1949, which came into force in 2001, mean that in England and Wales:

- Notice must be given **in person** by **both** parties to the marriage to the superintendent registrar at the register office in the district where you both live. If you live in the same district you should attend your local register office together to give notice. If you live in different districts then you must each give notice separately in your own district.

- Both of you must have lived in a registration district in England or Wales for at least seven days before giving notice of your intention to marry. You must give a minimum of 15 days' and a maximum of 12 months' notice of your intention to marry. If you make an advance booking more than one year ahead, it is essential that you also give formal notice as soon as you are legally able to do so.
- Each party to the marriage will be asked to declare his or her nationality.

When the superintendent registrar has accepted the notice, it is then entered into the marriage notice book and also displayed on a public notice board for 15 days. This provides the opportunity for anyone who has an objection to your proposed marriage to make a statement. After 15 days, you may apply for the certificate of authority for the marriage to proceed. This is not the same thing as a marriage certificate, which you can request after your wedding. If your notice of marriage is being displayed in two districts you must ensure both certificates of authority for the marriage are available prior to the wedding as you will be asked to produce them before the ceremony can go ahead.

The fee for giving notice is £30 each (i.e. £60 per couple), and at a register office you will also have to pay a fee of £34 to the registrar for attending your marriage, plus £3.50 for a marriage certificate which is issued after the ceremony, making a total cost of £97.50. At approved premises, as well as the £60 fee for giving notice, you will also have to pay a fee for the superintendent registrar and a registrar to attend. These fees are set by the local authority, and vary across the country. A charge will also be made for the use of the premises.

The date of your marriage can be set to take place at any time within a year of when the notice was given. If you find that you wish to postpone the wedding beyond that time you will have to apply and pay for a notice (or notices) again.

If you are marrying at a register office which is not in the district(s) where you reside, you should discuss making a provisional booking for the registrar of that district to attend your marriage, which can be confirmed when the certificate(s) of authority are issued.

Marriage in Scotland

For both civil and religious weddings in Scotland a minimum period of 15 days' notice must be given to the registrar in the district where the wedding is to be held, although four to six weeks' notice is preferred. Banns are no longer required for a religious ceremony. A schedule is then issued to the bride or groom up to seven days before the religious ceremony. It must be given to the minister before the service. For a civil wedding the schedule remains at the register office.

The order and content of the marriage service may be amended, and the minister or registrar may agree to the inclusion of non-scriptural readings of poems or prose. There is no residency requirement for marrying in Scotland.

Marriage in Northern Ireland

To be permitted to marry in a church, one of you must have been resident in a parish/district for seven days before giving notice of your intention to marry. To marry in a register office, one of you must have lived in a district for at least 15 days and the other for at least seven days.

Roman Catholic weddings

Anyone having a Roman Catholic wedding must give notice to the superintendent registrar (see pages 221–2), and in some cases the registrar must be present at the religious ceremony, though often the minister will be the registrar himself.

A Roman Catholic priest may insist on a lengthy period (usually at least six months) of notice of your intention to marry as it is regarded as essential for you to prepare properly for such a serious commitment. If the marriage is mixed (i.e. one of you is not Roman Catholic), the parish priest will have to apply for special permission on your behalf. Both ministers can attend the ceremony.

Jewish weddings

A couple wishing to marry in a synagogue should give notice of their intention to marry at a register office (see pages 221–2). The certificate or certificates of authority for marriage are issued to the secretary of the synagogue, and the declaratory and contracting words required to make the marriage legal are incorporated within the religious ceremony. Alternatively, couples may have a separate civil wedding at a register office, and a purely religious ceremony in the synagogue at another time. Jewish weddings can take place anywhere – in a synagogue, private house, hired hall or in the open air – as long as they are held under the *chuppah* or wedding canopy, which symbolises home, and the couple has the necessary legal document (certificate of authority for marriage, see page 222). The ceremony can be celebrated at any time, except during the Jewish Sabbath (from sunset on Friday until sunset on Saturday) or on festival or fast days. It must also be performed in the presence of 10 men, and two witnesses who are not related to either the bride or groom. Both the latter must be of the Jewish faith and free to marry. If either the bride or the groom is not Jewish, he or she must convert before getting married. The process is long and demanding, involving instruction and an examination. The groom must be a member of the synagogue in which the couple is to marry.

Nonconformist or Free Church, Muslim, Hindu and Sikh weddings

Nonconformist or Free Churches such as the Methodists, United Reformed Church, Baptists and Presbyterians and the Orthodox Church all require you to go to your local register office and apply to the superintendent registrar for a certificate of authority for the marriage to proceed. The same applies to Muslim, Hindu and Sikh weddings. Whether you will need a registrar to attend the religious ceremony itself depends on whether there is a person in your place of worship licensed to act as a registrar (this may be the minister or the priest) to witness your marriage. In addition to the 'authorised person' the marriage must be witnessed by at least two people.

Quaker weddings

The Religious Society of Friends★ (Quakers) has its own register-ing officers, who are allowed by law to witness the marriage and signing of the marriage certificate. Quakers wishing to get married must apply to the registering officer of the monthly meeting ('meeting' is the name given to the local Quaker community) of the area in which they intend to get married. Ideally, they should do this at least three months before the planned date (and cer-tainly no fewer than six weeks before). The couple must then complete a declaration of intention of marriage. All the legal requirements for a wedding in England and Wales or in Scotland must also be met. Notice of the intention to marry is then made public at the meetings.

The marriage of those not in formal membership is permitted, provided the couple are in sympathy with Quaker principles and practice, and they are known to, and their application to marry is supported by, local Quakers. Couples should consult the registering officer or a local overseer (responsible for pastoral care) and allow extra time.

Marriage certificates

On the day of your wedding at a register office or approved premises you can purchase a marriage certificate for £3.50. This is optional but a very useful document to have in your posses-sion. You will both be asked to disclose your addresses at the time of your marriage and your ranks or professions. The certificate also includes your natural or adoptive fathers' names as well as their ranks or occupations. If for any reason either of you does not wish to reveal this information there is no legal obligation to do so.

Divorce and remarriage

Whether you are allowed, as a divorcee, to remarry depends on the type of ceremony you wish to have.

Church of England

According to the regulations of the Convocations of Canterbury and York, 'the Church of England should not allow the use of the marriage service in the case of anyone who has a former partner still living'.

These regulations do not carry the weight of law but the majority of ministers object to divorced people marrying in church on moral grounds, even if the divorced partner is the innocent party. It is still worth discussing your hopes of marrying in church with your minister as in certain cases a service of blessing might be appropriate. Make it clear beforehand if you hope to have hymns, bridesmaids, flowers and wear traditional wedding clothes to your service of blessing as some ministers do not approve of this.

Civil weddings

You will need to provide proof of how the previous marriage ended. This could be a divorce absolute document, with the original court seal, or a death certificate or a certified copy; photocopies of these documents are not acceptable. In Scotland there is no equivalent to the decree nisi so you can remarry directly after the divorce is announced.

After taking personal details, the registrar will ask you to sign a declaration that you are eligible to marry. A false declaration could invalidate the marriage and may render you liable to prosecution under the Perjury Act, with the further possible offence of bigamy being taken into account.

Roman Catholic church

If either the bride or groom is divorced the couple are not permitted to have a Roman Catholic wedding; only those whose former partner is deceased or whose marriage was annulled (i.e. declared not to have been valid in the first place) can have a Roman Catholic ceremony.

Jewish faith

If either the bride or groom or both is divorced they must produce the decree absolute and the Jewish bill of divorce.

Quakers

Remarriage after divorce is a pastoral matter at the discretion of the local Quaker meeting, not a doctrinal issue.

Marrying abroad

Be sure to check all legal requirements for the wedding as they can differ from country to country. When looking through the brochure or making an initial enquiry check whether you need:

- a 10-year passport
- a visa
- your birth certificate
- return tickets to the UK
- your original decree absolute, if divorced
- original marriage certificate or former partner's death certificate
- parental consent if you are under 18 (21 in some countries)
- legal proof if your name has been changed by deed poll
- proof of vaccinations, if required
- if one of you is adopted, an adoption certificate.

If you require documents you should take originals, or copies certified by a notary, although some countries require you to send them in advance.

If your wedding is not being arranged through a travel agent check the minimum length of time you have to be resident as this can vary from two days to several months. Prior to leaving the UK find out from the consulate, embassy or High Commission of the country in which you wish to marry what the legal requirements are.

People you may not marry

It is forbidden in the United Kingdom for a man or a woman to marry certain blood relations. However, contrary to popular belief, first cousins are not prohibited from marrying. It is worth noting that some religions do not allow marriage between other relations.

Blood relatives

A man may not marry his: mother, sister, daughter, father's mother (paternal grandmother), mother's mother (maternal grandmother), son's daughter (granddaughter), daughter's daughter (granddaughter), father's sister (aunt), mother's sister (aunt), brother's daughter (niece), sister's daughter (niece).

A woman may not marry her: father, brother, son, father's father (paternal grandfather), mother's father (maternal grandfather), son's son (grandson), daughter's son (grandson), father's brother (uncle), mother's brother (uncle), brother's son (nephew), sister's son (nephew). These restrictions apply to half-blood relations and persons born out of wedlock.

Adopted relatives

If the adoption was authorised by an order of the court under the Adoption Act then the above restrictions apply. These are not removed even if another person has by a subsequent order been authorised to adopt the same person.

Step-relatives

Step-relatives aged 21 or more may marry provided that the younger member of the couple has at no time, before the age of 18, lived under the same roof as the older person. Neither must he or she have been treated as a child of the older person's family. Unless these conditions are met a man may not marry a: daughter of a former wife, former wife of his father, former wife of his father's father, former wife of his mother's father, daughter of a son of a former wife, daughter of a daughter of a former wife.

A woman may not marry a: son of a former husband, former husband of her mother, former husband of her father's mother, former husband of her mother's mother, son of a son of a former husband, son of a daughter of a former husband.

Relatives you may marry

The law was relaxed in 1960 to allow a man to marry his former wife's sister, aunt or niece and the former wife of his brother, uncle or nephew. Under previous legislation, these unions were prohibited unless the former spouse was deceased. The revisions in the law also apply to women.

The former spouses (in either or both cases) must be deceased if a man intends to marry the mother of a former wife or the former wife of a son, or if a woman intends to marry the father of a former husband or the former husband of a daughter.

Addresses

Association of Interchurch Families
35–41 Lower Marsh,
London SE1 7RL
Tel: 020-7523 2152
Fax: 020-7928 0010
Email: aife@msn.com
Website: www.aifw.org/aif/aif.htm

Baptist Union
Baptist House, 129 The Broadway,
Didcot, Oxfordshire OX11 8RT
Tel: (01235) 517700
Fax: (01235) 517715
Email: baptistuniontb@baptist.org.uk
Website: www.baptist.org.uk

Benefits Agency
Look in the phone book for your
local office

British Humanist Association
47 Theobalds Road,
London WC1X 8SP
Tel: 020-7430 0908
Fax: 020-7430 1271
Email: robert@humanism.org.uk
Website: www.humanism.org.uk
*Publishes a leaflet on humanist weddings
and a book, Sharing the Future, on
organising a humanist wedding*

Catholic Enquiry Office
The Chase Centre,
114 West Heath Road,
London NW3 7TX
Tel: 020-8455 9871
Fax: 020-8905 5780
Email: cms@cms.org.uk

Church of Scotland
Miss Susan Wilson,
121 George Street,
Edinburgh EH2 4YN
Tel: 0131-225 5722
Fax: 0131-220 3113
Website: www.cofs.org.uk

Contributions Agency
Look in the phone book for your
local office

Desktop Lawyer
www2.desktoplawyer.co.uk
*Online legal service. Prenuptial agreement
can be downloaded for £29.99, or £46.99
with legal phone support*

**Division of Ministries (Methodist
Overseas Division)**
Church House,
25 Marylebone Road,
London NW1 5JR
Tel: 020-7486 5502
Fax: 020-7935 1507

DVLA
Swansea SA1 1XX
Tel: (01792) 772151

Episcopal Church of Scotland
21 Grosvenor Crescent,
Edinburgh EH12 5EE
Tel: 0131-225 6357
Fax: 0131-346 7247
Email: office@scotland.anglican.org

Faculty Office of the Archbishop of Canterbury
1 The Sanctuary,
Westminster,
London SW1P 3JT
Tel: 020-7222 5381
Fax: 020-7222 7502

Family Planning Association Helpline
Tel: 020-7837 4044
Available 9am–7pm Monday–Friday for advice and information on all matters relating to contraception, sexual health and clinic details

Federation of Synagogues
65 Watford Way,
London NW4 3AQ
Tel: 020-8202 2263
Fax: 020-8203 0610
Email: info@kfkosher.org
Website: www.kfkosher.org

General Register Office for Scotland
New Register House,
Edinburgh EH1 3YT
Tel: 0131-334 0380
Fax: 0131-314 4400
Email: marriage@gros-scotland.gov.uk
Website:
www.open.gov.uk/gros/faq.htm
The website gives you all the information you need for marrying in Scotland, including a list of all the register offices and the documents needed for marriage, which you can download

General Register Office (Northern Ireland)
Registrar General,
Oxford House,
49–55 Chichester Street,
Belfast BT1 4HL
Tel: 028-9025 2028
Fax: 028-9025 2120
Website: www.nics.gov.uk/nisra/gro

General Synod of the Church of England
Enquiry Centre, Church House,
Great Smith Street,
London SW1P 3NZ
Tel: 020-7222 9011
Fax: 020-7222 6672
Website: www.cofe.anglican.org
The Enquiry Centre provides information about marriages in the Churches of England and Wales

Greater London Authority
43 Masham Street,
London SW1P 3PY
Tel: 020-7983 4000
Minicom: 020-7983 4458
Fax: 020-7983 4057
Email: mayor@london.gov.uk
Website: www.london.gov.uk

Guild of International Professional Toastmasters
12 Little Bornes,
London SE21 8SE
Tel: 020-8670 8424
Fax: 020-8670 0055
Email: ivor@ivorspencer.com
Website: www.ivorspencer.com

Hindu Society
673 Garratt Lane,
London SW17 0PB
Tel: 020-8944 0251

Incorporated Society of Valuers and Auctioneers
3 Cadogan Gate,
London SW1X 0AP
Tel: 020-7235 2282
Fax: 020-7235 4390
Website: www.isva.co.uk

Inland Revenue
Look in the phone book for your
local office

Jewish Marriage Council
23 Ravenshurst Avenue,
London NW4 4EE
Tel: 020-8203 6311
Fax: 020-8203 8727

Lesbian and Gay Christian Movement
Oxford House,
Derbyshire Street,
London E2 6HG
Tel/Fax: 020-7739 1249
Email: lgcm@aol.com
Send written request for details of ministers who are willing to conduct blessings for lesbian and gay couples

London Beth Din (United Synagogue)
Adler House,
735 High Road,
London N12 0US
Tel: 020-8343 8989
Fax: 020-8343 6257

Marriage Care (formerly the Catholic Marriage Advisory Council)
Clitherow House,
1 Blythe Mews, Blythe Road,
London W14 0NW
Tel: 020-7371 1341
Fax: 020-7371 4921
Email: marriagecare@btinternet.com

Methodist Church
1 Forest Gate, Central Buildings,
Westminster, London SW1H 9NH
Tel: 020-7222 8010
Fax: 020-7799 2152

Muslim Educational Trust
130 Stroud Green Road,
London N4 3RZ
Tel: 020-7272 8502
Fax: 020-7281 3457

Office for National Statistics
PO Box 56, Southport PR8 2GL
Tel: 0151-471 4817
Fax: 0151-471 4549
Website: www.ons.gov.uk
Send £5 for an up-to-date list of alternative licensed venues (payment by cheque, postal order, debit or credit card)

Pink Triangle Trust
34 Spring Lane, Kenilworth,
Warwickshire CV8 2HB
Tel/Fax: (01926) 858450
Email: GALHA@bigfoot.com
Website: http://visitweb.com/ptt

Premium Bonds Office
Blackpool, Lancashire FY3 9YP
Tel: (01253) 766151
Fax: (01253) 693182
Website: www.nationalsavings.co.uk

Pressed for Time (UK) Ltd
3 Swanwick Business Centre,
Bridge Road, Lower Swanwick,
Southampton,
Hampshire SO31 7GB
Tel: (01489) 574668
Fax: (01489) 574157
Will collect wedding bouquet from anywhere in the UK, photograph it, take it apart and create a picture of the bouquet using the petals and foliage

Reform Synagogues of Great Britain
The Sternberg Centre,
80 East End Road, London N3 2SY
Tel: 020-8349 4731
Fax: 020-8343 0901
Email: Admin@refsyn.org.uk
Website: www.refsyn.org.uk

Registrar General for England and Wales
Marriages Section,
General Register Office,
Smedley Hydro,
Trafalgar Road, Birkdale,
Southport PR8 2HH
Tel: (01704) 569824
Fax: 0151-471 4803
Website: www.ons.gov.uk
Advice and information about civil marriages in England and Wales

Relate
Herbert Gray College,
Little Church Street, Rugby,
Warwickshire CV21 3AP
Tel: (01788) 573241
Fax: (01788) 535007
Website: www.relate.org.uk
Offers courses on marriage preparation at some centres. Contact headquarters, or your local branch (number in phone book), for details

Religious Society of Friends (Quakers)
Friends House,
173–177 Euston Road,
London NW1 2BJ
Tel: 020-7663 1000
Fax: 020-7663 1001
Website: www.quaker.org.uk

Under Secretary of State
Nationality and Treaty Department,
Foreign and Commonwealth Office,
Clive House, Petty France,
London SW1H 9HD
For information on marriages abroad, and marriages to foreigners

Union of Liberal & Progressive Synagogues
The Montagu Centre,
21 Maple Street,
London W1P 6DS
Tel: 020-7580 1663
Fax: 020-7436 4184
Email: montagu@ulps.org

Unitarian and Free Christian Churches
Central Administration Office, Essex Hall, 1–6 Essex Street,
London WC2R 3HY
Tel: 020-7240 2384
Fax: 020-7240 3089
Email: ga@unitarian.org.uk
Website: www.unitarian.org.uk
May be able to supply details of ministers willing to conduct blessings for same-sex couples

United Reformed Church
86 Tavistock Place,
London WC1H 9RT
Tel: 020-7916 2020
Fax: 020-7916 2021
Email: urc@urc.kix.co.uk
Website: www.urc.org.uk

Wedding Crèche Service
1 Netley Mill, Shere,
Surrey GU5 9JT
Tel: (01483) 202490
Uses qualified staff to provide childcare and entertainment with toys, crafts, music and games

Designers and dressmakers

Bridal Wear by Design
Tel: (07990) 726402
Website:
www.bridalwearbydesign.co.uk

Designer Directory
Website: www.macculloch.com

Elegance Bridal Wear
Tel: (07990) 726402
Email:
info@elegancebridalwear.co.uk
Web site:
www.elegancebridalwear.co.uk

JMD Style
Tel: (07940) 773040
Email: jmd@jmdstyle.co.uk
Website: www.jmdstyle.co.uk

Marriages abroad: tour operators

Kuoni Weddings
Tel: (01306) 747007

Malta Tourist Office
Tel: 020-7292 4900

Thomas Cook
Tel: (01733) 418450

Thomson Weddings in Paradise
Tel: 0161-911 8338

Unijet Caribbean
Tel: (0990) 114114

Virgin Weddings
Tel: (01293) 744265
Includes Disneyland, underwater and helicopter weddings, as well as more conventional destinations

Passport offices

The helpline number for all offices is (0990) 210410. Calls are routed to the passport office that covers the area from which you are calling. Website (UK Passport Agency): www.open.gov.uk/ukpass/ukpass.htm
Has details of how to change your name on a passport and how to apply for a new passport

Belfast Passport Office
Hampton House, 47–53 High Street, Belfast BT1 2QS
Areas covered: All of Northern Ireland

Glasgow Passport Office
3 Northgate, 96 Milton Street, Cowcaddens, Glasgow G4 OBT
Areas covered: All of Scotland, Greater London and Middlesex

Liverpool Passport Office
5th Floor, India Buildings, Water Street, Liverpool L2 0QZ
Areas covered: Anglesey, Cheshire, Conwy, Cumbria, Denbighshire, Derbyshire, Durham, East Riding of Yorkshire, Flintshire, Greater Manchester, Gwynedd, Hartlepool, Kingston upon Hull, Lancashire, Merseyside, Middlesbrough, North East Lincolnshire, North Lincolnshire, Northumberland, North Yorkshire, Redcar, South Yorkshire, Staffordshire, Stockton-on-Tees, Tyne and Wear, West Yorkshire, Wrexham

London Passport Office
Clive House, 70 Petty France, London SW1H 9HD
Fax: 020-7271 8813 (to obtain leaflets)
This office deals with personal callers only from any part of the UK. Postal applications from residents of Greater London and Middlesex should be sent to the Glasgow office

Newport Passport Office
Olympia House, Upper Dock Street, Newport NP9 1XA
Areas covered: Bath and North East Somerset, Berkshire, Blaenau Gwent, Bridgend, Bristol, Caerphilly, Cardiff, Carmarthenshire, Ceredigion, Cornwall, Devon, Dorset, East Sussex, Gloucestershire, Hampshire, Hereford and Worcester, Isle of Wight, Monmouthshire, Merthyr Tydfil, Neath and Port Talbot, Newport, North West Somerset, Oxfordshire, Pembrokeshire, Powys, Rhondda Cynon Taff, Shropshire, Somerset, South Gloucestershire, Surrey (less London boroughs), Swansea, Torfaen, Vale of Glamorgan, West Sussex, Wiltshire

Peterborough Passport Office
Aragon Court, Northminster Road,
Peterborough PE1 1QG
Areas covered: Bedfordshire,
Buckinghamshire, Cambridgeshire, Essex
(less London boroughs), Hertfordshire
(less London boroughs), Kent (less
London boroughs), Leicestershire,
Lincolnshire, Norfolk, Northamptonshire,
Nottinghamshire, Suffolk, Warwickshire,
West Midlands

Photographs and videos

Association of Professional
Videomakers
Ambler House, Helpringham,
Lincolnshire NG34 0RB
Tel: (01529) 421717
Fax: (01529) 421742
Email: gerry@videomakers.com
Website: www.videomakers.com

Digital cameras: information
Website:
www.epicentre.co.uk/reports/
reports.html

Reviews of digital cameras
Guild of Wedding Photographers UK
Suite 16–17, Carlton Place,
22 Greenwood Street, Altrincham,
Cheshire WA14 1RZ
Tel/fax: 0161-926 9367
Email: news@gwp-uk.co.uk
Website: www.gwp–uk.co.uk

Master Photographers Association Ltd
Hallmark House, 2 Beaumont
Street, Darlington,
Co Durham DL2 5S2
Tel: (01325) 356555
Fax: (01325) 357813
Email:
enquiries@mpauk.demon.co.uk
Website: www.mpauk.demon.co.uk

Society of Wedding and Portrait
Photographers
5 Liverpool Road,
Ashton-in-Makerfield,
Wigan WN4 0YT
Tel: (01942) 711763
Fax: (01942) 725448
Email: derek@swpp.u-nt.com
Website: www.swpp.u-net.com

Publications

Inclusion in this list in no way
constitutes an endorsement by
Consumers' Association or Which?
Ltd, except in relation to its own
publications.
Gordon, K., 1998, *A Practical Guide to*
Alternative Weddings (Constable)
Ross-Macdonald, J., 1996, *Alternative*
Weddings: the Essential Guide
(Thorsons)
Simpson, J., 1998, *Noble's Wedding*
Venues Guide (Noble Publishing)

Wedding software

PC Wedding Kit
Includes database for keeping track
of guests, gifts and invitations and
enables you to produce your own
stationery. Made by MGI Software,
it costs £20 and is available from
Boots and Electronics Boutique.
Wedding Magic by FrogWare is a comprehensive wedding planner costing
£19.99. More details on www.frog-
waresoftware.com.

The Wedding Package from
www.artworksuk.com is a stationery
design package, with nine different
designs for producing co-ordinated
stationery, costing £19.95. Available
from Artworks, 3 Pond Side,
Wootton, Ulceby, N. Lincolnshire
DN39 6SF. Tel: (01469) 588138,
email: info@artworksuk.com.

www.itheeweb.com has a list of down-loadable software. The site also has details of how to create your own wedding web site

Wedding websites

Confetti
www.confetti.co.uk

Hitched
www.hitched.co.uk
Discussion forum, diary planner, wedding venues, speeches

Married 4 Ever
www.married4ever.co.uk
Directory of services, diary of wedding events and exhibitions, online wedding photo albums

Matrimonio
www.matrimonio.co.uk
Wedding co-ordinators

The Wedding List
www.theweddinglist.com
Merchandise and gift list

Wedding Guide UK
www.weddingguide.co.uk
Useful guide to all aspects of planning a wedding

Wedding Service
www.wedding-service.co.uk
Directory site, listing services and suppliers

Wedding Services 4 U
www.weddingservices4u.co.uk
Services directory and chat room

Weddings and brides
www.weddings-and-brides.co.uk
General wedding information on clothes, products and services

Weddings UK
www.weddings.co.uk
Guide to weddings on the Internet including a bulletin board where brides-to-be can exchange ideas.

Index

abroad, marrying 7, 25–6
  beach weddings 25, 26, 105, 107
  exotic wedding venues 25
  insurance 206
  legal requirements 25–6, 227
  limitations 26
  marriage certificates 25–6
  photography 26
  registering the marriage in the UK 26
  wedding organisers 57
  wedding packages 25, 26
address, notifying change of 62
adoption certificate 227
alternative ceremonies 7–8, 28, 31, 130, 151–3
annulment 226
approved licensed premises 7, 21–3, 143
  advantages 22–3
  bridesmaids and pages 79
  case history 149–51
  days and times 59
  details of 22
  flexibility 22, 59
  flowers 114

  music 129, 146
  non-religious ceremony 23
  personalising the ceremony 23, 146
  photography 139
  restrictions on 22
  Scotland 21–2
  second marriages 31
  wedding organisers 57
average age at marriage 8

banks
  joint/separate bank accounts 215–16
  personal loans 53–4
  wedding bank account 37
banns 39, 60, 220
  fee 220
  reading 62, 220
baptism certificate 219
Baptists 24, 162, 224
barn dance 196
beach weddings 26, 105, 107
beauty treatments 46, 61, 62
bells 60, 67, 127–8
best man 58, 74–6
  best woman 76

duties 63, 66, 67, 74–5, 119,
    121, 160, 161, 200, 201
gifts to 61, 63, 64, 79
more than one 75
outfit 61, 106
toasts and speech 193
birthstones 14
blood relations 227–9
bridal attendants 58, 76–7
chief bridesmaid 75, 77, 156
child attendants 38–9, 76–7,
    107
civil ceremonies 79
flower girls 77
flowers 110
gifts to 61, 63, 64, 79
matron of honour 76
outfits 46, 102, 107
page boys 107
transport to the church 119
bridal bouquet
hand-tied bouquet 110
pomander 110
preserving 112
tossing to the guests 112, 201
wired bouquet 110
budget 13, 35–49
average cost of a wedding 39
breakdown 39, 40, 46–9
checklist 41–5
contingency sum 35
discounts, negotiating 38
final budget 37
financing the wedding 50–5
overrunning 37
preliminary budget 35–7
records, keeping 37
sharing the costs 36–7
software packages 69

traditional responsibility for
    payment 36
written quotations 37
buttonholes and corsages 47,
    75, 76, 112

cake 39, 48, 131–4
cake boxes 131
cake cutting ceremony 191,
    195–6
cost 48
cost-cutting 133
as dessert 132
icing 133
making it yourself 60, 63,
    133
quantities 131, 132
shapes and decorations
    132–3
silk and sugar flowers 133
sponge cakes 132, 134
storing the top layer 132,
    134
tiered cake 131
cancellation 38, 202–3, 205
cars *see* transport
caterers 60, 178–81, 184
checklist 180–1
choosing 178–81
sample menus 178
catering 177–87
at home 182–4
average cost 48
buffet meal 178, 179
canapés and finger buffets
    179–80
cancellation 38
checklists 180–1, 183–4, 186
children's food 179

drinks 184–7
    extra costs 178
    portion sizes 180
    sit-down meal 179
    special dietary requirements 178
    VAT 38–9
    vegetarian options 179
ceilidh 196
ceremony *see* alternative ceremonies; civil ceremonies; religious ceremonies
certificates of authority for the marriage 222
checklists
    budget 41–5
    catering 180–1, 183–4, 186
    entertainment 199–200
    flowers 116–18
    gifts 96
    guests 91
    hotels 169–71
    music 130
    photographs and video 140, 142
    reception venues 168–71, 173–4, 175, 177
    transport 122
chief bridesmaid 75, 77, 156
    duties 77, 160
children
    activity crèche service 198
    bridal attendants 76–7, 107
    of previous marriages 30, 33
    and second marriages 33–4
    special roles 33–4
    wedding guests 82–3, 198
    witnesses 33–4

Church of England 23, 24, 154–61, 218, 220–1, 226
    service of blessing 31–2, 87
Church of Ireland 154
Church of Scotland 24, 154
Church in Wales 24, 154, 218
civil ceremonies 7, 8, 20–2, 20–3, 143–53
    15-day notice procedure 221–2
    bridal attendants 79
    case histories 146–51
    ceremony 144–5
    days and times 59
    fees 40
    flowers 113–14
    increasing numbers of 143
    legal requirements 7–8, 221–3
    marriage by certificate without licence 221–2
    music and readings 128–30
    non-religious nature 21, 128, 146
    outfits 105
    personalising 21, 146
    Scotland 22
    witnesses 79
    see also approved licensed premises; register offices
cladagh rings 15
clothes *see* outfits
complaints and compensation 208
computer
    wedding software 69–70
    see also Internet; wedding website
confetti 160, 201

confirmation certificate 219
contraceptive pill 61–2
credit cards 52–3
  additional cardholders 216
  protection 52–3

date and time, setting 59,
  219–20
deposits, loss of 203
diamonds 13–14
digital camcorders 73
digital photography 70, 71–2,
  135, 141
divorce 8–9, 17–18
  remarriage 225–7
  see also second marriages
dressmakers 98–101
  alteration of existing dress 101
  cost and payment 99, 100–1
  finding 99
  mail order service 99
  working with 99–100
drinks 184–7
  after the meal 185
  on arrival at the reception
    184
  checklist 186
  corkage fees 184
  cost 48
  cost-cutting 48, 185
  estimating quantities 187
  glass hire 185
  ice 186
  with the meal 185
  non-alcoholic drinks 184–5
  for the toasts 185

email address, notifying change
  of 65

engagement ring 13–14, 46
engagements 11–19
  breaking off 18–19
  formal announcements 12,
    30
  parties 13
  rings 13–14, 16
  second marriages 30–1
  telling parents and friends
    11
entertainment 196–200
  average cost 48
  checklist 199–200
  for children 198
  dancing 197–8
  ensembles and soloists 48,
    197
  non-appearance of 203
  orchestras, bands and groups
    48, 196–7
  recorded music, discos and
    DJs 48, 197
etiquette 10
exotic wedding venues 25

Family Planning Association
  Helpline 62
family planning clinic 61
father of the bride
  asking for permission to
    marry 11
  outfit 106
  speech 34
  step-father 78
father of the groom 106
favours 187
finances, joint 214–16
financing the wedding 50–5
  credit card payment 52–3

loans 51–5
  mortgage, increasing 54–5
  personal loans 53–4
  savings 50–1
fireworks 187
floral headdresses 47, 104, 112
florists 109–10, 114
  portfolio 109
flower girls 77
flowers 59, 61, 109–18
  average costs 47
  bridal attendants 110
  bridal bouquet 47, 110, 112
  buttonholes and corsages 47, 75, 76, 112
  checklist 116–18
  church flowers 47–8, 113
  civil ceremonies 113–14
  colour combinations 109
  cost 110
  floral headdresses 47, 104, 112
  florist 109–10
  hand-tied bouquets 110, 115
  hanging baskets 114, 176
  inspirational pictures 109
  pomander 110
  preserving the bouquet 112
  reception 47, 114
  seasonal flowers and their meanings 110, 111
  white flowers 109–10
  wired bouquet 110
foreigner, marrying a 26–8
  in a foreign country 27–8
  in the UK 27

gay and lesbian relationships 28–9

gifts 92–6
  between husband and wife 210
  checklist 96
  compiling 94–5
  delivery 92, 94
  displaying 95
  duplication 92, 94
  exchanging 94
  faulty goods 208
  insurance 203–4, 206, 207
  lists 60, 70, 92–3, 94–5
  making your own list 92–3
  money and vouchers 95
  price range 93
  returning 90
  second marriages 33
  security at reception 75, 95
  software packages (lists) 69
  store list 93
  tax-free gifts 210–11
  thank-you letters 60, 95
  to bridal party 61, 63, 64, 79
  to parents 80
glass hire 185
gloves 104
gold rings 14–15
groom
  speech 192–3
  wedding clothes 46, 61, 74, 75, 106–7
guests 81–96
  checklist 91
  children 82–3
  disabled and elderly guests 168
  former spouses 33
  guest list software packages 69

invitations 83–9
list-making 58, 81
overnight accommodation 60, 89
second marriages 33

hairdressing 46, 61
halls and function rooms 172
hats 104, 108
headdresses 47, 104, 112
Hindus 21, 164–5, 224
historical buildings as reception venues 173
honeymoon
    average cost 49
    cost-cutting 49
    going-away vehicle 75, 121
    insurance 207
    luggage 67, 74, 75
    passports and visas 60, 65–6
    paying for 52–3
    travel documents 66
    travel insurance 206, 207
    traveller's cheques and currency 63
    vaccinations 61
hotels
    checklist 169–71
    receptions 169–71
humanist ceremonies 152–3

insurance 60, 202–8
    all-risks extension 206, 207
    amount of cover 204
    borrowing against 54–5
    buying wedding insurance 204–5
    contents policy 206–7
    cost 49

dangerous sports 207
existing cover 205–7
home-based reception 204, 207
honeymoon 207
life insurance 216–17
loan protection insurance 54
loss-of-enjoyment factor 208
medical insurance 216
photographs and video 140
specialist policies 202–5
supplier failure 203, 208
travel insurance 206, 207
wedding cancellation 202–3, 205
Internet 9, 58, 68–70, 99
    downloading a pre-nuptial agreement 18
    wedding website 11, 60, 68–9
invitations 48, 60, 83–9
    checking the proof 88
    cost-cutting 48–9
    deadline for reply 84
    engraved 83
    flat printing 84
    formal weddings 83, 85–7
    former spouses 33
    hand-written envelopes 89
    informal weddings 87–8
    map and directions 89
    ordering time 60, 84
    pre-printed reply card 84
    quantity 84
    ready-printed 48–9
    second marriages 33
    sending 60, 89
    software packages 69, 83
    thermographic printing 83–4
    to reception only 87

wedding software packages
   83
wording 84–7

Jewish faith 24, 59, 87, 113,
   163–4, 224, 226

legal requirements 218–29
   15-day notice procedure 221
   Church of England weddings
      220–1
   civil weddings 221–3
   documents 219
   England and Wales 218–19
   Jewish weddings 224
   licences 58, 220–1
   marriage certificates 160, 225
   marrying abroad 25–6, 227
   Muslim, Hindu and Sikh
      weddings 224
   Nonconformist or Free
      Church weddings 224
   Northern Ireland 223
   parental consent 218
   prohibited marriages 227–9
   Quaker weddings 225
   remarriage 225–7
   Roman Catholic weddings
      219, 223
   Scotland 219, 223
   setting the date 219–20
Lent 59
Lesbian and Gay Christian
   Movement 29
licences 58, 220–1
   common licence 220–1
   special licence 59, 155, 221
life insurance 216–17
living together before marrying 8

loans 51–5
   credit cards 52–3
   from your insurer 54–5
   lenders 54
   loan protection insurance 54
   personal loans 53–4
   secured personal loans 54
London Partnerships Register
   28–9
lounge suits 106

make-up 61
manicure 62, 64
marital conflicts 9, 214
marquees 114, 115, 174–6
   checklist 175
   hanging baskets 114, 115, 176
   insurance 204
Marriage Act 1994 20, 143
marriage certificate 160, 162–3,
   225
   fee 39, 40
   marrying abroad 25–6
marriage preparation courses
   8–9
marriage statistics 8
matrimonial home 213
matron of honour 76
matt gold rings 15
medical insurance 216
Methodists 24, 162, 224
morning dress 61, 106
   accessories 106
   for children 107
mortgage, increasing 54–5
mother of the bride 67, 76,
   77–8, 108
   corsage 112
   outfit 108

role 77–8
transport to the church 119
mother of the groom 108
corsage 112
music and readings 123–30
alternative ceremonies 130
bells 60, 67, 127–8
checklist 130
civil ceremonies 128–30
compilation recordings 124
hymns and psalms 60, 123, 125, 127
non-religious 128–30
organ and choir 60, 67, 123–4
prelude 124
processional 124, 156
readings 128, 129–30
recessional 126
recorded music 125–6
religious ceremonies 123–8, 155, 156
while signing the register 125–6
Muslims 166, 224

newspaper announcements
engagement 12
marriage 62
second marriage 30
Noble's Wedding Venues Guide 22
Nonconformist (Free Church) 24, 162, 224
Northern Ireland 223
nuptial blessing 162
nuptial mass 161, 162

order of service sheets 48, 67, 75, 76, 127
copyright issues 127

layout 127
organisation 56–67
post-engagement decisions 57–9
setting date and time 59, 219–20
timetable 60–4, 66–7
on the web 58
wedding organisers 56–7
Orthodox Church 224
outfits 97–108
accessories 104
beach weddings 105, 107
best man 61, 106
bridal attendants 46, 102, 107
bride's mother 108
civil ceremonies 105
emergency repair kit 105
going-away outfit 46, 61, 67, 105–6
groom 46, 61, 74, 75, 106–7
hiring 46, 74, 103
loss or damage 203
lounge suits 106
second marriages 33
ushers 61, 74, 106
wedding dress see wedding dress and accessories

page boys 107
parents
bride's father 77, 156, 158, 192
bride's mother 67, 76, 77–8, 108
deceased parents 85–6
divorced parents 8, 10, 78, 85, 86, 189, 190
groom's parents 78

introducing 13
receiving line 78, 188–9
step-parents 78, 86, 190
parties
 engagement parties 13
 post-wedding parties 81
 stag and hen parties 62, 63,
  74, 76, 77
partnerships registers 28–9
passports and visas 60, 65–6
 amended passport 65
 new passport 65
pensions 212
periods 61, 62
personalising your wedding 7,
 8, 23, 145, 146
 at an approved venue 23, 146
 civil ceremony 21, 146
photographs and video 59, 62,
 75, 135–42
 albums 137–8
 amateur photography 136
 at the reception 136, 139, 189
 average costs 47
 checklists 140, 142
 in church 137, 138, 141
 customer dissatisfaction
  clause 141
 digital camcorders 73
 digital photography 70, 71–2,
  135, 141
 extra costs 138
 finding a photographer 135
 group photographs 137
 insurance 140
 marrying abroad 26
 package deals 136, 137–8, 141
 picture-editing software
  69–70

Polaroid shots 136
popular photographs 138–9
re-staging the wedding 204
reportage style 136
scanning in photos 70
special effects 138
style of photography 135–6
video 140–2
Pink Triangle Trust 29
platinum rings 15
post-nuptial agreements 8, 31
postponement 90
 notification of 90
pre-nuptial agreements 8,
 17–18, 209
 downloading 18
 emotional risks 18
 legalising 17–18
 prime function 17
 second marriages 31
Presbyterians 224
prohibited marriages 227–9
properties, selling 51

Quakers 24, 29, 59, 162–3, 225,
 227

readings 128, 129–30
reception 167–201
 average cost 48
 background music 196
 cake cutting ceremony 191,
  195–6
 cost-cutting 48
 entertainment 196–200
 flowers 47, 114
 food and drink 177–87
 halls 172
 home-based 176–7, 204, 207

hotels 168–71
leaving 121–2, 200–1
marquees 114, 115, 174–6, 204
organising 167–87
photography 139, 189
receiving line 75, 78, 161, 188–9
seating plan 34, 62, 63, 69, 189–91
second marriages 34
stationery and decorations 48, 187
time and duration 167
timetable 188
toastmasters 187, 191
toasts and speeches 34, 191–5
venue checklist 168–71, 173–4, 175
venue no longer available 203
venues 168–77
wedding book 90, 189
see also catering
register
music while signing 125–6
signing 79, 160, 162
witnesses 75, 77, 79, 160
register offices 21, 59, 81, 143–6
arriving at 143–4
bridesmaids and pages 79
choice of 21
fees 40
flowers 113–14
interview with registrar 144
music 128–9
non-religious ceremony 21, 146
personalising the ceremony 21

photography 139
registrar fee 144
size 81
websites 69
registrar, fees 40
Relate 8, 9, 214, 215
religious ceremonies 7, 8, 20, 59, 154–66
choice of service 155–6
Church of England 154–61
church fees 39, 63, 75
church flowers 47–8, 113
days and times 59
duration 156
form of service 60, 155–9, 220
Hindu 164–5
interfaith marriages 24
Jewish 163–4
legal requirements 7–8, 220–5
move away from 7, 143
music 60, 67, 123–8, 155, 156
Muslim 166
Nonconformist or Free Church 162
photography and 137, 138, 141
preparation sessions 23, 24, 154
promise to obey 156, 158
Quaker 162–3
readings 128, 155
rehearsals 60, 62, 63, 74, 154, 166
Roman Catholic 24, 161–2
in Scotland 23–4, 59
seating plan 159
second marriages 21, 32

service of blessing 31–2, 87
signing the register 160, 162
Sikh 165–6
wording 23
residency requirement 32, 223
restaurant reception venues 172, 173
rice 160
rings 13–17, 60
  alternatives to 17
  antique rings 15, 205
  average cost 46–7
  best man's care of 75
  birthstones 14
  caring for 16–17
  custom-made 15
  engagement rings 13–14, 46
  engraving 15
  exchanging 145, 158–9, 162
  gold and other metals 14–15
  interlocking 15
  men's rings 16, 46
  no legal obligation to exchange 145
  returning 19
  valuations and insurance 16–17, 203, 205
  wedding rings 14–15, 16
Roman Catholics 24, 161–2, 219, 223, 226
rose gold rings 15
Russian wedding rings 15

Sale of Goods Act 1979 208
same-sex partnerships 28–9
savings and investments 211
Scotland
  approved licensed premises 21–2

civil weddings 22
  legal requirements 219, 223
  religious ceremonies 23–4, 59
  second marriages 32, 226
  wills 214
seating plans
  church weddings 159
  reception 34, 62, 63, 69, 189–91
second marriages 8, 10, 30–4, 225–7
  ceremonies 31–2
  changing your surname 31
  children of previous marriages 30
  choice of venue 31
  church weddings 21, 32, 226
  civil weddings 226
  financial implications 31
  formal announcements 30
  invitations 33
  involving your children 33–4
  outfits 33
  reception 34
  Scotland 32, 226
  service of blessing 31–2
  speeches 34
  wedding gifts 33
  wills and 31
service of blessing 31–2, 87
ship, marrying on board 22
shoes 61, 101, 104
signet rings 15
Sikhs 21, 165–6, 224
silver rings 15
speeches 63, 75, 191–5
  best man 193
  bride 193

bride's father 192
duration 191
groom 192–3
jokes 194
nerves 191
planning and delivering 194–5
second marriages 34
websites 69
stag and hen parties 62, 63, 74, 76, 77
stationery
average cost 48–9
order of service sheets 61
reception 48, 187
software packages 69
see also invitations
step-parents 78, 86, 190
step-relatives 228
supplier failure 203, 208
Supply of Goods and Services Act 1982 208
surname
changing to husband's surname 31, 64
composite surnames 64
informing others 62, 65
keeping maiden name 64
man's change of 64
and second marriages 31

taxation 209–11
capital gains tax 210, 211
inheritance tax 210
marriage and 209–10
savings and investments 211
tax-free gifts 210–11
themed weddings 7, 23, 105
timetable 60–4, 66–7
contingency time 188

toastmaster 58, 187, 191
toasts 191–5
transport 58, 64, 67, 119–22
average costs 47
borrowing cars 120–1
checklist 122
decorations 120
going-away vehicle 75, 121
horse-drawn carriages 121
leaving the reception 121–2
non-appearance of 203
open-topped cars 121
parking arrangements 75, 121
seatbelts 120
stylish alternatives 122
timing the journey to the church 63
to church 75, 119
to the register office 119
vintage and veteran cars 120
wedding cars 47, 119–21

umbrellas 104, 120
Unitarian and Free Christian Church 29
United Reformed Church 24, 162, 224
ushers 67, 74, 75
duties 76, 127, 160
number of 76
outfits 61, 74, 106

vaccinations 61
VAT 38–9
veils 103–4
full-length veil 103–4
lifting back 156
short veil 104

video *see* photography and video
vows, personalising 145

wedding book 90, 189
Wedding Crèche Service 198
wedding day timetable 66–7
wedding dress and accessories
  97–105
  average cost 46, 50
  bridal fabrics 101, 103
  buying 97–8
  cleaning and storing 103
  end-of-season bargains 98
  evening gowns 98
  fittings 61, 62, 100, 101
  gloves 104
  having a dress altered to fit
    101
  hiring 46, 103
  made-to-measure 46, 98–103
  mail order service 99
  secondhand 46, 98, 101
  shoes 61, 101, 104
  tights and stockings 104
  train 100, 103
  umbrellas 104
  underwear 61, 101, 104
  veils, headdresses and hats
    47, 61, 103, 112
wedding night 60
wedding notebook 58
wedding organisers 56–7
  approved licensed premises 57

finding 57
functions 57
overseas tour operators 57
wedding promises 28
wedding rings 14–15, 46
wedding website 11, 60, 68–9
  chat room 71
  content and quality 68
  cost 71
  creating your own 69, 70–3
  directory sites 69
  features 70
  File Transfer Protocol (FTP)
    program 71
  general information sites 68
  name, choosing and
    registering 71
  photos and video clips 72–3
  specialised sites 69
  webcams 73
white gold rings 15
wills 212–14
  made in contemplation of
    marriage 213
  revocation by marriage 212
  in Scotland 214
  second marriages and 31,
    213
winter weddings 59
witnesses 75, 77, 79, 218, 219
  children 33–4
  civil ceremonies 79
  religious ceremonies 160

WHICH? BOOKS

The following titles were available as this book went to press.

General reference (legal, financial, practical, etc.)

Be Your Own Financial Adviser	432pp	£9.99
420 Legal Problems Solved	352pp	£9.99
150 Letters that Get Results	336pp	£9.99
What to Do When Someone Dies	176pp	£9.99
The Which? Computer Troubleshooter	192pp	£12.99
The Which? Guide to an Active Retirement	530pp	£12.99
The Which? Guide to Changing Careers	352pp	£10.99
The Which? Guide to Choosing a Career	336pp	£9.99
The Which? Guide to Choosing a School	336pp	£10.99
The Which? Guide to Computers	352pp	£10.99
The Which? Guide to Computers for Small Businesses	352pp	£10.99
The Which? Guide to Divorce	368pp	£10.99
The Which? Guide to Doing Your Own Conveyancing	208pp	£9.99
The Which? Guide to Domestic Help	208pp	£9.99
The Which? Guide to Employment	304pp	£10.99
The Which? Guide to Gambling	288pp	£9.99
The Which? Guide to Getting Married	224pp	£9.99
The Which? Guide to Giving and Inheriting	256pp	£9.99
The Which? Guide to Going Digital	272pp	£10.99
The Which? Guide to Home Safety and Security	198pp	£9.99
The Which? Guide to Insurance	320pp	£10.99
The Which? Guide to the Internet	320pp	£10.99
The Which? Guide to Money	448pp	£9.99
The Which? Guide to Money on the Internet	256pp	£9.99
The Which? Guide to Pensions	336pp	£9.99
The Which? Guide to Renting and Letting	336pp	£10.99

The Which? Guide to Shares	288pp	£9.99
The Which? Guide to Shopping on the Internet	272pp	£10.99
The Which? Guide to Starting Your Own Business	288pp	£10.99
The Which? Guide to Working from Home	256pp	£9.99
Which? Way to Buy, Own and Sell a Flat	288pp	£10.99
Which? Way to Buy, Sell and Move House	320pp	£10.99
Which? Way to Clean It	256pp	£9.99
Which? Way to Drive Your Small Business	240pp	£10.99
Which? Way to Manage Your Time -- and Your Life	208pp	£9.99
Which? Way to Save and Invest	464pp	£14.99
Which? Way to Save Tax	320pp	£14.99
Wills and Probate	224pp	£10.99
Make Your Own Will	28pp	£10.99

Action Pack (A5 wallet with forms and 28-page book inside)

Health

Understanding HRT and the Menopause	256pp	£9.99
The Which? Guide to Children's Health	288pp	£9.99
The Which? Guide to Complementary Medicine	270pp	£9.99
The Which? Guide to Managing Asthma	256pp	£9.99
The Which? Guide to Managing Back Trouble	160pp	£9.99
The Which? Guide to Managing Stress	252pp	£9.99
The Which? Guide to Men's Health	336pp	£9.99
The Which? Guide to Personal Health	320pp	£10.99
The Which? Guide to Women's Health	448pp	£9.99
Which? Medicine	544pp	£12.99

Gardening

The Gardening Which? Guide to Growing Your Own Vegetables	224pp	£18.99

The Gardening Which? Guide to		
Patio and Container Plants	224pp	£17.99
The Gardening Which? Guide to		
Small Gardens	224pp	£12.99
The Gardening Which? Guide to		
Successful Perennials	224pp	£17.99
The Gardening Which? Guide to		
Successful Propagation	158pp	£12.99
The Gardening Which? Guide to		
Successful Pruning	240pp	£12.99
The Gardening Which? Guide to		
Successful Shrubs	224pp	£12.99

Do-it-yourself

The Which? Book of Do-It-Yourself	320pp	£14.99
The Which? Book of		
Plumbing and Central Heating	160pp	£13.99
The Which? Book of Wiring and Lighting	160pp	£16.99
Which? Way to Fix It	208pp	£12.99

Travel/leisure

The Good Bed and Breakfast Guide	640pp	£14.99
The Good Food Guide	736pp	£15.99
The Good		
Skiing and Snowboarding Guide	592pp	£15.99
The Good Walks Guide	320pp	£13.99
The Which? Guide to Country Pubs	576pp	£13.99
The Which? Guide to Pub Walks	256pp	£9.99
The Which? Guide to Scotland	528pp	£12.99
The Which? Guide to Tourist Attractions	544pp	£12.99
The Which? Guide to		
Weekend Breaks in Britain	528pp	£13.99
The Which? Hotel Guide	752pp	£15.99
The Which? Wine Guide	512pp	£14.99
Which? Holiday Destination	624pp	£12.99

Available from bookshops, and by post from:
Which?, Dept TAZM, Castlemead,
Gascoyne Way, Hertford X, SG14 1LH
or phone FREE on (0800) 252100
quoting Dept TAZM and your credit-card details

Which? Holiday Destination

An A–Z guide to where to go on holiday

Brochures from tour operators are colourful and enticing, and travel books are fine once you have decided where you're heading – but this guide to holiday destinations worldwide is the only one that summarises the key facts that tell you whether you will enjoy being there.

Which? Holiday Destination is a country-by-country guide to the most popular holiday venues around the world. It includes forthright thumbnail descriptions of resorts and the range of activities on offer to help you decide whether that resort is somewhere to take the family or to have a romantic break away from it all.

Weather charts are provided for each country, together with information on when to go, the packages available and the type of accommodation you could expect when you get there. The book also includes a holiday checklist, tips on health and safety abroad, web sites and a list of tour operators.

Paperback   210 x 120mm   624 pages   £12.99

Available from bookshops, and by post from
Which?, Dept TAZM, Castlemead,
Gascoyne Way, Hertford X, SG14 1LH
or phone FREE on (0800) 252100
quoting Dept TAZM and your credit card details

Which? Way to Save and Invest

With an estimated 30,000 financial products now on the market, among them many based on the performance of the ever-proliferating 'dot.coms', what chance do you have of making an informed choice which will ensure that your money works for you?

Fully revised and updated, *Which? Way to Save and Invest* helps you to choose a reliable home for your money, whether it is £50 or £50,000.

This no-nonsense, accessible guide shows you how to formulate a strategy that suits your financial circumstances and how to put it into effect, with or without an adviser, via traditional routes or the Internet. It assesses the vast range of financial products, including bank and building society accounts, National Savings, with-profits products, the new breed of income bonds, other tax-efficient investments, annuities, pensions (including stakeholder), shares, and ethical and 'alternative' investments.

Paperback   210 x 120mm   352 pages   £14.99

Available from bookshops, and by post from
Which?, Dept TAZM, Castlemead,
Gascoyne Way, Hertford X, SG14 1LH
or phone FREE on (0800) 252100
quoting Dept TAZM and your credit card details

The Which? Hotel Guide

'The bible of good service.'   *Channel 5*

Idyllic inns, converted castles, family-friendly farmhouses, business bases – *The Which? Hotel Guide* has them all. It offers a choice of over 1,000 places throughout England, Scotland and Wales, so it will help you pick the ideal accommodation whether you want a country retreat, a luxurious spot for a romantic break, a hotel with conference facilities or a good base for a family holiday.

Completely rewritten every year, *The Which? Hotel Guide* offers colourful descriptions of each hotel's facilities, atmosphere and food, which pick out any special or quirky aspects unique to the hotel or its owners. Proudly independent, the Guide selects on the basis of professional inspection and readers' reports.

In addition to providing up-to-date prices and practical information on individual hotels, the Guide:
- highlights **fine food, peaceful locations** and **good value**
- includes 3 '3 nights for the price of 2' vouchers
- contains easy-to-read colour maps and photographs of award-winning hotels
- takes no advertising or payment for inclusion and accepts no free hospitality.

Paperback   210 x 120mm   752 pages   £15.99

Available from bookshops, and by post from
Which?, Dept TAZM, Castlemead,
Gascoyne Way, Hertford X, SG14 1LH
or phone FREE on (0800) 252100
quoting Dept TAZM and your credit card details

Which? Way to Clean It

Most people hate cleaning, but find the sight of greasy kitchens, grubby lavatories and grimy carpets deeply depressing. *Which? Way to Clean It* shows how to do the job as quickly and efficiently as possible. It is the ultimate handbook for people who care for their home and possessions but resent the time lost to the scourer or the duster.

This new edition tells you how to clean everyday household items, from microwave ovens to car windscreens; banish mould and mildew; treat stubborn stains and ground-in substances; care for valuable and delicate articles, from silk to jewellery and antiques; keep on top of the dirt by establishing an easy cleaning routine; make effective use of commercial cleaning products – the ones that really do a useful job; and find out which old wives' remedies really work.

The book also covers care of personal items, as well as getting to grips with outdoor cleaning and eliminating household pests. In addition, it offers lots of tips – from removing make-up and alcohol stains from clothes, to cleaning for babies and elderly people and dealing with fire or flood damage. Plus: an extensive address list will put you in contact with specialist cleaning services, as well as listing hard-to-obtain products which may be available only by mail order.

Paperback   216 x 135mm   256 pages   £9.99

Available from bookshops, and by post from
Which?, Dept TAZM, Castlemead,
Gascoyne Way, Hertford X, SG14 1LH
or phone FREE on (0800) 252100
quoting Dept TAZM and your credit card details